...ERS
IN MEIRIONNYDD

Circular Walks in Meirionnydd

Dorothy Hamilton

ISBN: 0-86381-545-5

Cover design: Alan Jones

Cover photo: Pont Llaeron

First published in 1999 by
Gwasg Carreg Gwalch, 12 Iard yr Orsaf, Llanrwst, Wales LL26 0EH
☎ 01492 642031   🖷 01492 641502
✆ books@carreg-gwalch.co.uk   Internet: www.carreg-gwalch.co.uk

Other title by the same author:

CIRCULAR WALKS ON ANGLESEY

Gwasg Carreg Gwalch, £4.50

Contents

LOCATION MAP

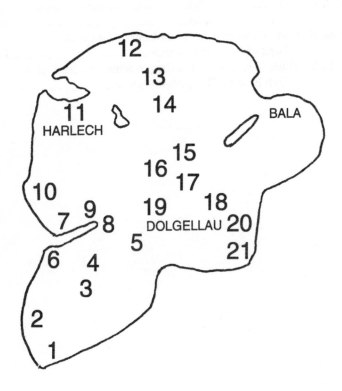

Introduction

Walks in this guide range from 2 hour easy rambles to whole day mountain routes. The walks selected highlight Meirionnydd's beautiful, varied landscape and historical interest. Several of the walks are rewarding to naturalists.

Easy to follow directions and sketch maps are provided for every walk. The starting points are at, or near, a car park or parking place. Directions are given to reach the start by car and, where possible, by public transport. Bus timetables that also give train information are available from Tourist Information Centres.

The walks are graded according to length and terrain. Very few walks in Meirionnydd are flat! Easy walks have low mileage and ascents are gentle or short. Moderate walks have longer uphill sections. Walks classed as strenuous reach the mountain tops. The average time taken to complete each walk is given, but extra time may be needed for food breaks, photography, bird watching etc. The best Ordnance Survey maps to use are the 1:25 000 Outdoor Leisure Series: the maps nos. 18 (Harlech and Bala) and 23 (Cadair Idris) cover all but one of the walks. Points of interest are included for each route, and these give background information relating to the landscape and historic sites of the area. Facilities list alternative parking, public toilets, pubs, cafes and places to visit.

The majority of walks do not pass refreshment places; therefore on the longer routes, or if there are children in the group, it is a good idea to take some food and drink for a snack along the way. All the walks require sturdy footwear, and boots are advisable on the mountains. Take care – choose good weather for the high level walks, and be prepared by carrying extra clothing.

Background

The name Meirionnydd comes from Meirion, a grandson of Cunedda, who founded a dynasty between the Dyfi and the Mawddach in the 5th century. This area became part of the ancient kingdom of Gwynedd. Nowadays, Meirionnydd encompasses the southern area of Snowdonia and its coast, stretching from the Afon Glaslyn near Porthmadog to Aberdyfi in the south, and inland to the east of Bala.

Most of the land is mountainous, cut by river valleys and estuaries. The most popular mountain, but not the highest in southern Snowdonia, is Cadair Idris. Its long ridge, seen on a clear day from the Mawddach or the Panorama Walk, impels even the most casual of walkers to attempt its summit. Aran Fawddwy, the highest peak in Meirionnydd, attracts smaller numbers, but those reaching the ridge of this shy mountain can truly feel that they are on top of the world.

Beneath the mountains, innumerable lakes nestle in secret corries or lay desolate on lonely plateaus. Legends of fairies and monsters, giants and King Arthur ring true in these remote settings.

Meirionnydd is well known for its waterfalls, and since tourists first came here, waterfalls have been on most itineraries. Thomas Love Peacock visited Rhaeadr Ddu (Ganllwyd) by moonlight. If possible, take a waterfall walk after heavy rain.

Only a few remnants of the native oak woodlands remain. Coed Ganllwyd and Coed Garth Gell are examples of the sessile oak woodlands that were once the main habitats on the hillsides of Meirionnydd. Farmers cleared the wooded valleys, and the remaining oaks on the slopes were gradually felled for house and ship building. Fortunately, some landowners thought to enhance their estates with trees, especially around Dolgellau. Coniferous tree planting started in the 1920s, and the vast Coed-y-Brenin Forest grows on hillsides that were once covered with native oak, birch and ash. The forest, however, does retain a herd of fallow deer from the Vaughan Estate.

In the forest, the Afon Mawddach plunges as a fall, and flows on to reach the sea near Barmouth. Possibly the most beautiful of all estuaries, the Mawddach is the gem of Cardigan Bay. Penmaenpool at the head of the estuary, has a wildlife information centre in the old signalbox of the former railway line. Parts of the old rail track are in the walk from Penmaenpool, and also the one starting at Morfa Mawddach.

North of the Mawddach, the wild Rhinog mountains display the oldest rocks in Snowdonia. These are the sediments laid down during the geological Cambrian age, about 600 million years ago. Earth movements during the Devonian era uplifted North Wales above the sea to form the arch of the Harlech Dome, the Rhinogydd. The intermediate Ordivician and Silurian deposits have since eroded to expose the Cambrian rocks. The Ordovician period was a time of great volcanic activity when igneous rocks intruded into sedimentary rock, and magma erupted and cooled on the surface. The volcanoes have since been covered with sediment and then folded, faulted, uplifted and eroded to form the mountains of Cadair Idris, Aran, Arenig, Manod and Moelwyn – known as the 'ring of fire'.

The Ice Ages began over one million years ago, and did not come to an end until about 10,000 BC. Ice 300 metres thick covered the mountains, and glaciers spread into the valleys. Those that moved westwards gouged out the present day estuaries. The effects of glaciation are evident and dramatic in this part of Snowdonia. The mountain sides have been hollowed to form corries and lakes, backed by sheer cliffs, such as at Llyn Cau and Llyn y Gadair under Cadair Idris.

At the end of the Ice Age, the sea level was lower than it is now and the coastline was several miles further west. Windblown seeds colonised the fertile glacier debris, and developed into grassland and forests of birch, willow, alder and pine. As the sea level rose, the forests were submerged – across the Dyfi estuary to the south of Ynyslas, stumps of ancient trees can be seen on the beach. And the coastline continues to change: the rock on which Harlech castle was built in the 13th century, at that time overlooked the sea. Between Harlech and Barmouth, a bank of stones known as Sarn Badrig (St Patrick's Causeway) starts a mile offshore, and continues south-west for over twelve miles. If man-made, it must be evidence of past land in Cardigan Bay.

Little is known of early man in Meirionnydd until the arrival of the New Stone Age (Neolithic) people, who built tombs to bury their dead. On the slopes of the Rhinog mountains, close to Dyffryn Ardudwy, graves of the type known as *portal dolmens* can be found. Similar designs are also found on the east coast of Ireland. Later,

11

Bronze Age man travelled along trackways marked by standing stones through the Rhinog range and Cadair Idris foothills. Burial monuments in the form of cairn circles from this age can still be seen, including the impressive Bryn Cadair Faner above Talsarnau.

Celtic speaking people first came to Meirionnydd from Central Europe about 600BC, during the Iron Age. They built defensive hill-forts, but lived in farmsteads, and centred their lives around agriculture. Then came the Roman invasion, and parts of North Wales were controlled from the legionary fortress at Chester, and the garrison at Segontium near Caernarfon. The most interesting Roman site in Meirionnydd is at Castell Tomen y Mur near Maentwrog, where the fort has two stages of development, and includes an amphitheatre, bath-house and parade ground. Nearby at Sarn Helen, the Roman road from Canovium near Conwy passes the fort, on its journey to Maridunum near Caerfyrddin. Another road came from Segontium, and ran eastwards to Caer Gai near Bala. Near Dolgellau there is a small fort at Brithdir. Remains of Roman tile kilns can be seen above the Rhiw Goch holiday village near Trawsfynydd.

About the time of the Roman withdrawal, the chieftain Cunedda and some of his tribe came south from Hadrian's Wall to defend Wales against the Irish. Cunedda's grandson Meirion gave his name to Meirionnydd, and his descendants continued to rule the district for many generations. This was the Dark Ages, when Wales was divided into small kingdoms. The only remains from this period are Christian stones. 5th-7th century stones with inscriptions are to be seen at Llanaber church, south of Barmouth, and in the parish church of St Cadfan, Tywyn, which is the earliest example of written Welsh.

In the early years of the 12th century, a castle was built at Cymer at the confluence of the Mawddach and Wnion rivers. This was destroyed by Einion ap Gruffudd when Meirionnydd became part of the kingdom of Powys. After Einion's death in 1123, the district came under the rule of Gwynedd. A Cistercian abbey was founded at Cymer about 1189 by Maredudd ap Cynon, who was a grandson of Owain Gwynedd. The monks kept sheep, reared horses and engaged in mining and metallurgy. At the time of the Dissolution, the monks – or possibly thieves – hid a silver gilt chalice and paten from the abbey on a nearby hillside. They lay hidden under boulders until the 19th century, when they were accidentally found by gold miners returning home to Llanfachreth.

At the beginning of the 13th century, Llywelyn ap Iorwerth became the most successful and powerful of the medieval Welsh princes, and by the time of his death, he ruled most of Wales. He constructed a number of castles, including Castell y Bere. After his death, his grandson Llywelyn ap Gruffudd eventually became the ruler, and he was acknowledged as the Prince of Wales by Henry III. However, Llywelyn underestimated the son of Henry, England's next king, Edward I. Conflict between them culminated in war, and Llywelyn was killed near Builth Wells. Llywelyn's death brought an end to Welsh independence and his kingdom was divided into English type shires. Meirionnydd, Ardudwy and Penllyn were combined to form Merionethshire. The district of Mawddwy was not included in the county until the Acts of Union, under Henry VIII.

Harlech was one of the castles built by Edward I to consolidate his victory in North Wales. There is no evidence of a previous castle or court apart from in the story of Branwen in the Mabinogion. A translation of this old legend is available from most bookshops in Wales. Harlech Castle took only seven years to build and the architect, as with Edward's other castles in North Wales, was Master James of St George. At that time the rock was approachable from the sea, and a watergate with a path of over 100 steps led to an upper gate and drawbridge.

The castle withstood the rising of Madog ap Llywelyn in 1294, but was taken by Owain Glyndŵr in 1404. It became his home and headquarters, where he held council with his supporters. The castle was heavily besieged in 1408, when Glyndŵr's wife and two of his daughters were taken prisoner. During the Wars of the Roses the castle was held for the Lancastrians, and Henry VI's queen Margaret of Anjou found refuge here. Defended for the king in the Civil War, Harlech was the last castle to be lost to the Parliamentarians.

The first discovery of gold in Meirionnydd is lost in the distant past. The Romans may have known about the presence, but there is no evidence of Roman mines. The monks of Cymer Abbey had mineral rights which reverted to the Crown at the Dissolution. Gold was rediscovered in the 1830's and by the middle of the century, the Meirionnydd gold rush was under way. Clogau and Gwynfynydd were the most important mines, although there were many smaller ones. The lodes, however, were unreliable and the mines became unprofitable and eventually closed.

Although slate was used for floors and roofing from the Roman period or earlier, it was not commonly used until the 16th century. During the late 18th century it became an organised industry, and the town of Blaenau Ffestiniog developed solely because of the success of the quarries in the area. Transport of slate was by pack animals and carts until the opening of the Ffestiniog Railway in the 1830's. The Talyllyn Railway, from Nant Gwernol to Tywyn, improved the efficiency of the Bryneglwys quarry near Abergynolwyn. Both the Ffestiniog and Talyllyn Railways are now very successful tourist attractions.

The building of the Barmouth railway viaduct across the Mawddach estuary opened up the Cambrian Coast line. Rail and road networks led to an increase in tourism, and it is now one of the main industries in Snowdonia. Apart from the seaside resorts and a few small inland towns, Meirionnydd remains a sparsely populated hill farming area.

Welsh Place-names

The following words are used in place-names in Meirionnydd.

Aber – *estuary, river mouth*
Aderyn (Adar) – *bird(s)*
Afon – *river*
Bach/Fach – *small*
Blaen – *head (of valley)*
Braich – *arm*
Brith – *speckled*
Bryn – *hill*
Bwlch – *pass*
Bychan – *little*
Cadair – *chair*
Cae – *field*

Caer/Gaer – *fort*
Canol – *middle, centre*
Capel – *chapel*
Carreg – *stone*
Castell – *castle*
Cau – *hollow or enclose*
Cefn – *ridge*
Celli/Gelli – *grove*
Ceunant – *ravine*
Clogwyn – *cliff*
Coch – *red*
Coed – *wood/trees*

Craig – *rock*
Croes – *cross*
Cwm – *valley*
Cymer – *confluence/junction*
Dinas – *fort*
Dôl/Ddôl – *meadow*
Drws – *door*
Du/Ddu – *black*
Dwr – *water*
Dyffryn – *valley/dale*
Eglwys – *church*
Enw(au) – *name(s)*
Esgair – *ridge/esker*
Ffordd – *road*
Ffridd – *mountain pasture*
Ffynnon – *spring, well*
Gafr – *goat*
Gallt/Allt – *hillside/slope*
Garn – *cairn*
Garth – *hill or enclosure*
Glan – *riverbank*
Glas – *blue*
Gwaun/Waun – *moor*
Gwyn – *white*
Hafod/Hafoty – *summer dwelling*
Hen – *old*
Hendre – *winter dwelling*
Isaf – *lower*
Llan – *church*
Llechwedd – *hillside/slope*
Llety – *lodging/inn*
Llwyd – *grey*
Llyn – *lake*
Llys – *court, palace*
Maen – *stone*
Maes – *field*
Mawr/Fawr – *big, great, large*
Melin – *mill*
Moel/Foel – *bare hill/mountain top*

Morfa – *marsh*
Mynach – *monk*
Mynydd/Fynydd – *mountain*
Mur – *wall*
Nant – *stream*
Newydd – *new*
Ogof – *cave*
Pandy – *fulling-mill*
Pant – *hollow, valley, dent*
Parc – *park, field*
Pen – *head, top*
Pentre – *village*
Pistyll – *spout, cataract*
Plas – *mansion*
Pont – *bridge*
Pwll – *pool*
Rhaeadr – *waterfall*
Rhiw – *hill*
Rhos – *moorland, heath*
Rhyd – *ford*
Sarn – *causeway, road*
Siglen – *swamp, bog*
Tir – *land*
Tomen – *mound*
Traeth – *beach*
Traws – *across*
Tref – *town*
Trwyn – *promontory*
Ty – *house*
Tyddyn – *small-holding, small farm*
Uchaf – *upper*
Uwch – *above, higher*
Y/Yr – *the*
Ynys – *island*

Walk Reference Guide

The following lists are a quick guide to the different types of walks in this book, and their historic interest. The walks in the natural history list visit reserves and other places of interest to naturalists.

Mountain Walks: 3, 5, 20
Moorland and Hill Walks: 7, 8, 10, 11, 12, 21
Woodland and Forest Walks: 9, 15, 16, 18, 21
Waterfall Walks: 6, 13, 15, 16
Lakeside Walks: 1, 2, 6, 12, 17
Estuary Walks: 6, 8, 9
Natural History Walks: 2, 6, 8, 9, 16, 17

Prehistoric and Roman
Sites: 6, 10, 11, 13, 14
Churches, Castle: 2, 4, 18, 19
Gold Mines: 9, 15, 16, 21
Slate Quarries: 3, 12, 14, 21

Information Centres

Aberdyfi Tourist Information	01654 767321
Bala Tourist Information Centre	01678 521021
Barmouth Tourist Information Centre	01341 280787
Blaenau Ffestiniog Tourist Information Centre	01766 830360
Corris Tourist Information Centre	01654 761244
Dolgellau Tourist Information Centre	01341 422888
Harlech Tourist Information Centre	01766 780658
TywynTourist Information Centre	01654 710070
RSPB Wales Office	01686 626678
Weathercall	0891 500415

Country Code

1. Guard against any risk of fire.
2. Keep to the public rights of way when crossing farmland.
3. Avoid causing any damage to walls, fences and hedges.
4. Leave farm gates as you find them.
5. Keep dogs under control and on leads in the presence of livestock.
6. Leave machinery, farm animals and crops alone.
7. Take care not to pollute water.
8. Carry your litter home with you.
9. Protect all wildlife, plants and trees.
10. Avoid making any unnecessary noise.
11. Drive carefully on country roads.
12. Enjoy and respect the countryside.

Aberdyfi – Cwm Maethlon (Happy Valley) – Llyn Barfog (Bearded Lake) – Aberdyfi

OS Maps:	1:50 000 Landranger Sheet 135; 1:25 000 Outdoor Leisure Sheet 23.
Start:	The car park on the sea front in Aberdyfi, G.R. 612959.
Access:	Aberdyfi is on the A493, 10 miles from Machynlleth. Trains on the Cambrian Coast Line stop here. Bus 29 from Tywyn or Machynlleth.
Parking:	On the sea front, near the beach, in Aberdyfi.
Grade:	Moderate – paths, tracks and lanes.
Time:	4-4½ hours.

Points of Interest:

1. Aberdyfi is an attractive seaside village at, as the name suggests, the mouth of the Dyfi estuary. Nowadays well known for its sailing, the village has an impressive maritime history. Herring was landed here, and barley and wheat were imported. In the 18th century, oak bark, timber and wool were exported. Forty ships were built here in the mid 19th century, when Aberdyfi became the port for the Dyfi valley following the development of local copper, lead and slate mines. The legend of Cantre'r Gwaelod tells of how a fertile valley, reputedly close by in Cardigan Bay, was inundated in the 6th century, at the time of Gwyddno Garanhir. The land of Cantre'r Gwaelod was drowned when the sea broke through the defensive walls. 'The Bells of Aberdovey', a song written for the opera 'Liberty Hall' by Charles Dibdin in 1785, refers to church bells below the sea near Aberdyfi. (The village did not have a church at that time.) There are numerous reports of the sound of bells on windless nights.

2. Many legends surround the hillside lake, Llyn Barfog. The name (Bearded Lake) may refer to the water lilies that grow here in summer.

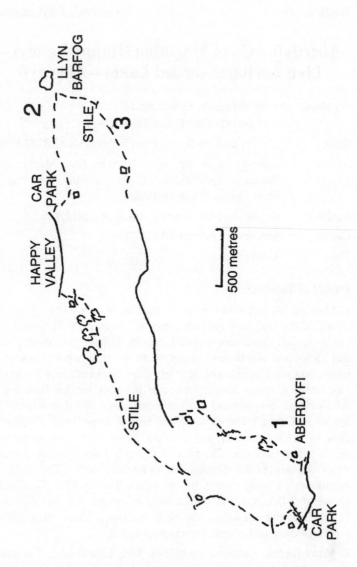

500 metres

LLYN BARFOG

STILE

2

3

CAR PARK

HAPPY VALLEY

STILE

ABERDYFI

1

CAR PARK

One story associates the lake with the water monster Yr Afanc, which was removed either by King Arthur or Hu Gadarn (Hu the Mighty), and dragged to Llyn Cau beneath Cadair Idris (see Walk 5). Another legend says that Llyn Barfog is the home of Gwyn ap Nudd, the King of the Fairies. It is said that long ago on summer evenings the fairies, dressed in green, could be seen along the banks of the lake with their greyhounds and white cattle. A local farmer captured one of the fairy cows and she gave an enormous quantity of rich creamy milk, and gave birth to many wonderful calves. She became famous in the neighbourhood and made the farmer wealthy. However, when the cow became old, he foolishly arranged for her to be slaughtered. On the appointed day, the butcher set about to kill the fairy cow, but as he raised his knife, he and the farmer were struck motionless. A lady dressed in green robes appeared calling the cow's name, and the cow and all her progeny filed up the hill. When the farmer and butcher were freed from the spell, they rushed after them and were just in time to see the herd disappear into the lake. Neither the cattle nor the fairies were ever seen again.

3. The stone inscribed *Craig Carn March Arthur* refers to the rock nearby, indented with the mark of a horse's hoof. The impression is said to have been left by King Arthur's horse after it leapt across the Dyfi estuary, to escape pursuing enemies.

Walk Directions: (-) denotes Point of Interest

1. From Aberdyfi (1) car park, turn left along the A493 and pass under the railway bridge. Immediately, turn right on a path that runs alongside the railway line.

2. Before reaching a house, turn left on a path uphill. Pass a house on the left, and continue on a track until it reaches a road junction.

3. Cross the road to a stile, and turn right on a path along the hillside. Where the path forks, take the higher path and emerge in a field. Keep walking ahead, with an overgrown path below on the right. At the end of the field, cross a ladder stile and follow the track to a lane.

4. Keep ahead uphill. Go through a gate, and pass a reservoir on the right. Where the lane bends left, turn right on a stony track and follow

this to a lane.

5. Turn left and ignore the lane on the right. In a few paces, where the lane bends right to a cattle grid, keep walking ahead on a path to a gate. Go through a second gate, and follow the enclosed path to a field.

6. Keep ahead to a pair of gates. Go through the left hand gate, and follow the right-hand fence to the next gate. Keep ahead across an open field, and descend to reach a fence corner on the left.

7. Bear half right, slanting downhill on a path into the valley. Near the corner of the field, at a stream and gates, cross a ladder stile.

8. Follow the left fence and join a track. Continue with a fence on the left, soon going downhill and through a gate into woodland. Cross a footbridge and continue over a stile. Pass houses on the left and reach the lane in Cwm Maethlon (Happy Valley).

9. Turn right, and go uphill to a car park on the right. Go through the car park and a kissing-gate. Turn left on the track, and follow it towards a farm. Just before the house, turn left to a ladder stile.

10. Continue on a track, and cross another stile. Just before a stream, turn right on a path uphill. Cross the stream, join a track and continue walking uphill to a stile. Pass through a reedy area to cross another stile, and walk towards Llyn Barfog (2).

11. Take a path that bears right, uphill and away from the lake. Ignore tracks on the left, and veer right to climb a ladder stile. Continue on the track and just before a wall on the left, look for an inscribed slate (3).

12. Continue on the track. It bears right, and at a cottage go through the left-hand gate. Keep ahead on the track, which becomes a lane with magnificent views over Happy Valley.

13. After crossing a cattle grid, the lane starts to descend. Views of the Dyfi estuary open up. Turn left on a tarmac track and pass through a gate. In another 60 metres, reach two gates on the right.

14. Go through the second gate and follow the left fence for about thirty metres, towards buildings. Now bear right, descending across the

middle of a field, aiming for a gap in some bushes, to the left of a telegraph pole.

15. In the next field descend diagonally left, but before the far corner go through a gap into the adjacent field on the left. Follow the right hedge to a path leading to stiles and a stream.

16. Turn left to another stile and keep ahead to a gate. Follow a narrow path above a valley to another gate. Continue above trees and bear right, shortly crossing slates, towards a telegraph pole.

17. About twenty metres before the pole, turn left and follow a path to a stile. Descend through gorse and brambles to some steps. Pass a house on the left, and reach a lane.

18. Turn right, and in a few metres bear left on a path. Descend past houses to the A493. Turn right to the starting point.

Facilities:

Car park in Cwm Maethlon. Public toilets near the Tourist Information Centre in Aberdyfi. Pubs and cafes in Aberdyfi. There is a weekly market in Machynlleth, and a Nature Reserve at Ynyslas on the opposite side of the Dyfi estuary.

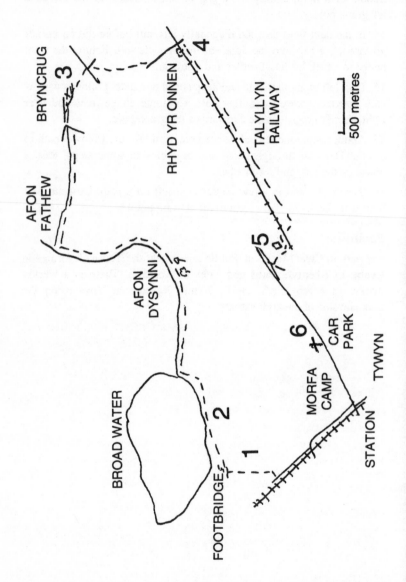

BROAD WATER

FOOTBRIDGE

AFON DYSYNNI

AFON FATHEW

BRYNCRUG

RHYD YR ONNEN

TALYLLYN RAILWAY

MORFA CAMP

CAR PARK

STATION

TYWYN

500 metres

1
2
3
4
5
6

22

Tywyn – Broad Water – Afon Dysynni – Bryncrug – Rhyd-yr-onnen – Tywyn

OS Maps:	1:50 000 Landranger Sheet 135; 1:25 000 Outdoor Leisure Sheet 23.
Start:	The crossroads near the Cambrian Coast line railway station in Tywyn. G.R. 583007.
Access:	Tywyn is on the A493, 14 miles from Machynlleth. Trains on the Cambrian Coast line stop here. Buses 29 and 30 from Machynlleth. Bus 28 from Dolgellau.
Parking:	Several car parks in the town.
Grade:	Easy/Moderate – level walking beside lake and river, field paths, some road.
Time:	3½-4 hours.

Points of Interest:

1. RAF Tywyn opened at Tonfannau, in September 1940 to provide air target training facilities. It became No. 631 Squadron in 1943, after the U and C Flights of No. 1 AACHU had moved in with Queen Bees and Hawker Henleys, and amalgamated. The airfield had problems with winter water-logging, and the squadron moved to Llanbedr in 1945.

2. Broad Water is a fine place for bird watching. Heron, shelduck, merganser, mallard, oystercatcher, redshank, dunlin and other waders may be spotted. Cormorants may also be seen flying up the Dysynni valley to Craig y Deryn (Bird Rock), where there is an inland cormorant colony.

3. Mary Jones was born in 1784 at Tyn-y-ddôl in Llanfihangel-y-Pennant and, when she was sixteen, she made the long walk to Bala to get a Bible. It had taken Mary several years to save the money, and because she had only one pair of shoes, she allegedly walked barefoot

most of the way. When Mary arrived at the home of Thomas Charles, the Bibles had not arrived. After waiting for them, Mary was rewarded with three Bibles for the price of one. Mary's story deeply affected Mr Charles, and as a result of his persuasion the Religious Tract Society established the British and Foreign Bible Society in 1804. Shortly afterwards the society published Welsh Bibles for use in Sunday Schools. Mary married Thomas Lewis, a weaver, and they lived at Bryncrug. They had six children. Mary died in 1864 and she is buried in the graveyard of Capel Bethlehem at Bryncrug.

4. Talyllyn Railway was built in the 1860's for the carrying of slate from quarries near Abergynolwyn. The 2ft 3in gauge railway connected with the main line railway on the coast at Tywyn. It opened in late 1866, and the following year saw passenger as well as freight services on the line. Sir Haydn Jones was the last private owner, and when he died in 1950 there was a possibility of the line closing. A group of railway enthusiasts formed a preservation society and the volunteers have re-laid the track, strengthened bridges and rebuilt stations. Trains now run from Easter to October, and at Christmas.

5. Y Groes Faen standing stone is about seven or eight feet high and has a broken top. Its significance is unknown. It could be a prehistoric stone marking a route, a Christian stone or a farmpost! According to local legend, long ago, a dragon terrorised the district with its flames, but after people prayed for several successive nights at the cross it disappeared.

6. St Cadfan is said to have arrived in Tywyn in the 6th century, having travelled by sea from Brittany. Cadfan is also believed to be the founder of the monastery on Ynys Enlli (Bardsey Island). With his brothers, he settled near the well (now somewhere under a garage near the high street) and led a simple life centred around prayer, study and the growing of food. The church grew and became the Mother Church of the area. Early buildings were of wood – Vikings burnt two of them – and the present church was built in the 12th century. The most important thing to see is the Cadfan Stone. The two inscriptions on the stone are in Welsh, and are thought to be the oldest written example of the language, from the 5th to 7th century. The stone was found about

half a mile from the church in the 17th century, and had been used as a gatepost. Also of interest in the church are two 14th century effigies. One, known as the Crying Knight, sheds tears in wet weather. Much of the church is modern, but the nave is 12th century.

Walk Directions: (-) denotes Point of Interest

1. Starting from the crossroads near the main line station in Tywyn, take the road for Morfa Camp. After passing the camp, the road reaches a level crossing. Do not cross, but bear right and 60 metres beyond the last house, turn right on a track.

2. Go through a gate, and turn left in another twenty-five metres on a track. Follow it through the old airfield (1) for about 400 metres to a tall pole, which is a footpath signpost.

3. Turn left for a few paces, and then right to cross a footbridge over a wide channel. Follow a path diagonally right to Broad Water (2). Continue, with the lake on your left.

4. Cross a stile and follow the embankment. Continue beside the river, Afon Dysynni, and ignore all foopaths leading off. In about 2.5km, the path leaves the Dysynni and bears right on an embankment beside a narrower river, Afon Fathew. Follow it to a kissing-gate at a road and bridge, on the A493 at Bryncrug.

5. Cross the road and turn left. In a few paces, turn right in the direction of Talyllyn. Pass a bus shelter on the right, and reach a ladder stile at the Recycling Centre. Continue another forty metres to Capel Bethlehem if you wish to see Mary Jones' Grave (3).

6. Retrace your steps and cross the ladder stile. Turn left on a clear path with the river on your right. Pass behind the chapel, go through a field and continue through a gap in a hedge. Cross the footbridge over the river, and keep ahead.

7. Ignore the kissing-gate ahead, and turn sharply left on a path. Pass a house on the right, cross a bridge over a stream, and follow a track to a road.

8. Cross the road to the lane ahead. In fifty metres, climb a stile on the right. Follow the narrow enclosed path to a field, and continue near the

left hedge and fence to a stile in a corner. Keep a fence and stream on your right to reach the next stile. Go ahead following the stream to a footbridge, and you soon reach a stone stile at a lane.

9. Turn left and pass a camp site on the left. Ignore a stile on the right, and cross the bridge over the Talyllyn Railway (4) at Rhyd-yr-onnen Station. Cross a ladder stile on the right, and keep ahead through gates. Go over a track and continue with the railway line nearby, on the right.

10. When the track bears left uphill, stay near the right fence. Leave the next field by a gate, some distance from the railway line. Continue through another gate and bear right to a bridge over the railway line.

11. Go through two farmyard gates, passing a house on the right. Turn right through another gate onto a track that passes the house, Hen-dŷ, on its right. Continue to a lane and turn right to meet another lane. (Continue ahead if you wish to see Y Groes Faen (5), which is behind a wall just before the main road.)

12. Turn left to the main road, A493. Keep left, and follow the pavement past a garage and St Cadfan's Church (6), to the starting point in Tywyn.

Facilities:

Alternative car park in Bryncrug. Public toilets near the station in Tywyn. Pubs in Tywyn and Bryncrug. Several cafes in Tywyn. Talyllyn Railway. Several campsites in the area.

Abergynolwyn – Nant Gwernol – Bryneglwys – Pont Llaeron – Tarren y Gesail – Abergynolwyn

OS Maps:	1:50 000 Landranger Sheet 124, 135; 1:25 000 Outdoor Leisure Sheet 23.
Start:	Car park opposite the Railway Inn at Abergynolwyn. G.R. 677069.
Access:	Abergynolwyn is on the B4405 between Tywyn and Minffordd. Bus 30 from Tywyn or Machynlleth. Nant Gwernol is the terminus for the Talyllyn Railway.
Parking:	Small car park near the shop in Abergynolwyn.
Grade:	Strenuous – woodland, moorland and grassy mountain paths. Forest track and lane.
Time:	5½-6 hours.

Points of Interest:

1. Abergynolwyn has only existed, as a village, since the mid 19th century. Until the development of the Bryneglwys Quarry it consisted of two small hamlets, Pandy and Cwrt, with a total of 15 houses, chapel, inn, mill and tannery. Pandy is Welsh for a fulling-mill, and this would have been sited near the river. Cwrt goes back to the Middle Ages, and is at the end of Llanegryn Street (the road to Castell-y-Bere), on the far side of the bridge crossing the Afon Dysynni. The two rivers, Nant Gwernol and Afon Dysynni, meet near Cwrt and used to form a whirlpool.

2. Nant Gwernol is the terminus of the Talyllyn Railway. The 2ft 3in gauge line was built for the purpose of transporting slate to the main line in Tywyn, and the port of Aberdyfi. Packhorses carried the slate to Pennal before the opening of the line in 1866. The following year,

Abergynolwyn – Nant Gwernol – Bryneglwys – Foel Llechwedd-du – Tarren y Gesail – Abergynolwyn

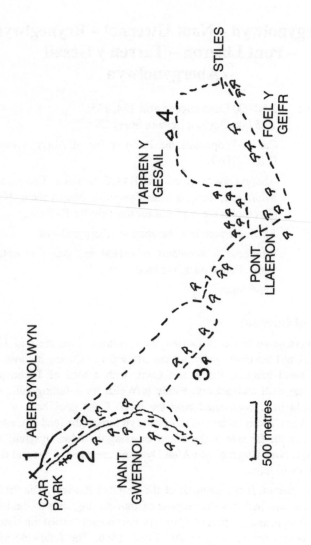

passenger services ran from Abergynolwyn station to Tywyn. After the closing of the quarries and the death of the last private owner, Sir Haydn Jones in 1950, a railway preservation group took over the railway. Nant Gwernol station opened in 1976, the railway previously terminating in Abergynolwyn Station. Across the bridge is the Alltwyllt incline which connected the railway to the slate quarries. Dippers and grey wagtails may be seen in the stream.

3. Early in the 19th century Bryneglwys quarry operated on a small scale. In 1865, Lancashire cotton mill owners bought the quarry and made extensive developments, building several mills and a network of inclines and tramways. At the end of the century, nearly 300 men were employed and output was around 8000 ton each year. Sir Haydn Jones bought the mill and the Talyllyn Railway in the early years of the 20th century. After the World Wars quarrying became unprofitable, and the mine closed in 1947. The majority of the buildings have been demolished. Across the valley of Nant Gwernol is the Beudynewydd incline, and below in the storage yard are the remains of the turbine mill. Further on, the ruins of the manager's house is passed on the left.

4. The Tarren hills are never crowded, and often give clear views when Cadair Idris has a blanket of cloud. From Tarren y Gesail (2186ft) on a fine day the views are magnificent with Cadair Idris to the north-east, Tarren Hendre on the west and Pumlumon in the distant south.

Walk Directions: (-) denotes Point of Interest

1. Starting from Abergynolwyn (1) car park, take the lane alongside it. Beyond the houses, the lane goes uphill to reach a footpath signpost on the right for Nant Gwernol Station. Take this path and follow the river on your right, but ignore the bridge to the station (2).

2. Continue beside the stream, Nant Gwernol, and pass a number of small waterfalls. Cross a footbridge at the meeting of the streams, Nant Gwernol and Nant Moelfre. At a path junction, bear left through woods to follow blue topped posts. The path eventually makes a sharp right turn, and goes uphill to a track.

3. Turn left uphill on the track. In about 350 metres, at a fork, go left

downhill. The track crosses Nant Moelfre and bends left. After a right bend, ignore a track descending on the left. Tips of the disused Bryneglwys quarry (3) can be seen from the track.

4. Follow the main track to a gate and stile. Keep a fence on the left to reach another stile. Keep ahead, and in about 120 metres, at a signpost, turn right on a narrow footpath.

5. Follow the path through coniferous trees and reach a small gate. Keep ahead with a fence nearby (at first), and cross a boggy section, where the path is faint in places. Sundew may be found here. Reach coniferous trees and a fence on the left, cross a stile, and follow a path to the old packhorse bridge, Pont Llaeron.

6. Cross the bridge, and bear slightly right uphill on a narrow path to reach coniferous trees. Keep ahead on a clear path, bearing left through a gap in the trees, then right again steeply uphill. When the trees end, ascend to a stile.

7. Bear left to cross a ladder stile. When the right-hand fence bears away downhill, continue along the ridge of Foel y Geifr, keeping a fence nearby on the left. Ignore a couple of stiles in the fence.

8. After about 1.5km., the fence turn sharp right to descend. Here, cross a stile and follow a fence on the left. In 300 metres, four fences meet on a col. Keep ahead and pass two stiles on your left. (These provide an escape route to Pont Llaeron.)

9. Follow the fence on your left up the steep slope, to where three fences meet. Cross the fence on your left, pass a cairn, and follow a fence on the right to the trig point on Tarren y Gesail (4).

10. Keep ahead, west, on a faint path. In 400 metres, the path bears left to descend the mountain shoulder. Tarren Hendre is directly ahead. Reach a forest and follow its fence on your right, downhill. Ignore a gate, but continue descending to the bottom edge of the forest.

11. Turn right through a gate and walk along a path below the forest. It passes above Pont Llaeron and reaches the outward route that leads to the bridge, near the stile crossed earlier. Retrace your steps to the signpost at the quarry track.

12. Turn right, and shortly pass a large pit on the right. In about 600

metres join another track. Turn left downhill, pass below the ruins of Hendrewallog, and follow the lane to the car park in Abergynolwyn.

Facilities:

Public toilets near the start at the rear of the car park. Shop and Railway Inn at Abergynolwyn. Campsites in the area. Talyllyn Railway. Short waymarked trails from Nant Gwernol Station. Dolgoch Falls.

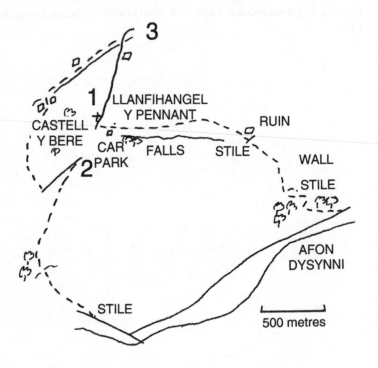

3

1 LLANFIHANGEL
Y PENNANT

CASTELL
Y BERE

RUIN

CAR
PARK

FALLS

STILE

WALL

2

STILE

AFON
DYSYNNI

STILE

500 metres

Llanfihangel-y-Pennant – Dysynni Valley – Castell y Bere – Mary Jones' Cottage – Llanfihangel-y-Pennant

OS Maps:	1:50 000 Landranger Sheet 124; 1:25 000 Outdoor Leisure Sheet 23.
Start:	Car park opposite Llanfihangel church. G.R. 672088.
Access:	Leave the A487 at Minffordd and follow the B4405 to Abergynolwyn. Take the Llanegryn road and in 2.5km turn right past Castell y Bere. From the coast, leave the A493 at Bryncrug or Llanegryn and follow minor roads past Castell y Bere to Llanfihangel. The nearest bus stop is at Abergynolwyn.
Parking:	Car park opposite Llanfihangel church.
Grade:	Moderate – paths and lanes.
Time:	3-3½ hours.

Points of Interest:

1. Dedicated to St Michael, the church dates back to the 12th century. Inside there is a very old font, and on the north side of the church look for the leper's window. Lepers were not allowed in the church, but could follow the service through the window.

2. The romantic stronghold of Castell y Bere was built by Llywelyn ap Iorwerth (Llywelyn the Great) in 1221. He was succeeded by his grandson, Llywelyn ap Gruffudd, who was killed in 1282 by the English. Dafydd, the brother of Llywelyn, had established himself here at Castell y Bere, but fled into the mountains before the English took the castle in April 1283. Dafydd was caught and executed that summer, and Castell y Bere became an English garrison. Edward I usually established towns around castles, but if he had such plans in this valley they did not materialize. The Welsh captured the castle in

1294 under Madog ap Llywelyn, but since then it appears to have been abandoned. Excavations revealed decorated tiles and stained glass windows. From the ruins there are fine views west of spectacular Craig y Deryn (Bird Rock) where cormorants fly inland to breed.

3. Mary Jones, in 1800, walked barefoot to Bala, hoping to purchase a Bible. She had learnt to read by attending a Circulating School in Abergynolwyn, which had been set up by Mr Thomas Charles of Bala. Wanting a Bible of her own, she had saved what she could from her small earnings, and took six years to reach the purchase price of three shillings and sixpence. The route Mary took was probably past Rhiwogof (see Walk 5), above Talyllyn, up the pass and through the Wnion valley. When Mary arrived in Bala, Mr Charles had no Bibles. According to one story, he had sold out and gave her his last copy. Another version relates that the Bibles had not arrived, and Mary was sent to a servant's house until they came. Thomas Charles then gave her three Bibles for the price of one. He was so impressed by Mary's fortitude that he persuaded the Religious Tract Society to form the British and Foreign Bible Society. Mary married Thomas Lewis, a weaver, and they had six children but only one survived. This son, John, emigrated to America. Mary was 80 when she died, and her grave may be seen in Capel Bethlehem's graveyard at Bryncrug (see Walk 2).

Walk Directions: (-) denotes Point of Interest

1. Opposite the church (1), take a footpath which goes alongside the car park. Pass a house and ruins on the right, and cross a ladder stile. Follow the path above the stream and after passing waterfalls, bear left uphill to a stile in the fence.

2. Turn right to walk beside the stream and ignore a stile on the right. The valley widens, and the path veers away from the stream to reach a wide track, which it follows for a short distance before going through a gate. Keep ahead to some ruins, cross a stream and go over a ladder stile.

3. Continue uphill on a green path. Go through a very wide gap in a wall, and here bear right to follow the wall to a track and a stile at a gate.

4. Descend the track, and in about 180 metres turn right on a narrow path. Follow it downhill through trees to a stile at the edge of the woods. Continue over a ladder stile and keep walking ahead to a stile in the left corner of a field.

5. Turn right on a quiet lane through the Dysynni valley, and continue for about two kilometres to a junction. Turn right and walk uphill. In 400 metres, as the lane starts to make a long descent, look for a narrow path on the right going up to a stile and footpath signpost.

6. Follow the path, which rises gently to the left along the hillside. In 300 metres pass some slabs of rock and a few trees on the right. Keep ahead, descending slightly, to cross a stile above trees.

7. Cross a stream and follow a wall on the left. Descend beside it until an arrow points to the right around an outcrop. Go right, but descend to find a clear path again, above a wall on the left.

8. Ignore a gate on the left, but continue to a junction of fences and cross a stile to the left of a gate. Follow a good path descending gradually along the hillside in the direction of Castell y Bere (2).

9. Reach a wider track and turn right. In about 200 metres go through a kissing-gate on the left. Slant half-right across the field to a stile at the lane. (To visit Castell y Bere, go right for 100 metres along the lane to a kissing-gate.)

10. Turn left along the lane, and in 300 metres cross a stile on the right. Follow the fence on the left, shortly bearing right to pass the craggy hill. When the crags end, continue beside the left-hand fence to a ladder stile.

11. Follow a fence on the right to a broad metalled gate, and emerge on a track. Turn left past barns, and left again to pass a farmhouse on the right. Go through a gate, and keep ahead to a bridge over Afon Cadair. Turn right on a path alongside the river.

12. Keep ahead, crossing stiles and reach a track. Pass a house on the left and continue beside the river to a lane. The ruins of the cottage where Mary Jones (3) was brought up can be seen on the opposite side of the road. Turn right to cross the bridge and follow the lane to the church and car park.

Facilities:

Toilets at the start in the trees near the car park. Railway Inn at Abergynolwyn. Tearoom at Llanegryn. Campsites in the area. Craig y Deryn. Talyllyn Railway.

Minffordd – Llyn Cau – Craig Cau
– Cadair Idris – Hafoty Gwastadfryn
– Pencoed – Minffordd

OS Maps:	1:50 000 Landranger Sheet 124; 1:25 000 Outdoor Leisure Sheet 23.
Start:	Dôl Idris car park near Minffordd, G.R. 732115.
Access:	Leave the A487 at Minffordd on the B4405. The car park is shortly on the right. Buses to the road junction from Machynlleth, Dolgellau and Tywyn.
Parking:	Dôl Idris car park, Minffordd.
Grade:	Strenuous – woodland and hill paths, some stony. Tracks.
Time:	5 hours to the summit and back. 7-8 hours for the circular walk.

Points of Interest:

1. The Minffordd path from Dôl Idris is probably the shortest route up Cadair Idris. Although strenuous and steep, it is not difficult and five year old children reach the summit. The full circular walk covers a variety of terrain, and at twelve miles may be too long for some people. In this case, simply retrace your steps from the summit to the car park.

2. Enclosed on three sides by precipitous cliffs, Llyn Cau is a fine example of a corrie lake. For thousands of years the basin was gouged by a glacier which left behind its terminal moraine to act as a dam. The cwm is part of the Cadair Idris Nature Reserve, and many Arctic Alpine plants can be found here. According to tradition, the lake is home to a monster, because either King Arthur or Hu Gadarn (see Walk 1) dragged the afanc from Llyn Barfog to Llyn Cau. A local

37

Minffordd – Llyn Cau – Craig Cau
(Cadair Idris – Mynydd Moel)
Pencoed – Minffordd

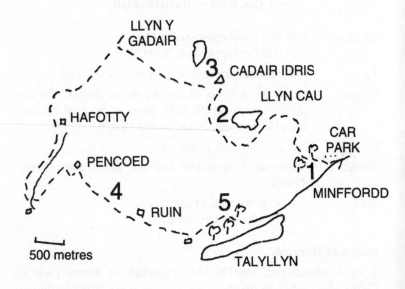

story relates that in the 18th century, a boy was seized by a monster as he swam across the lake.

3. From the summit of Cadair Idris – Penygadair – if you are lucky enough to have clear weather, the views can encompass the Mawddach estuary, the Rhinogydd, Aran, Arenig, Tarren and Pumlumon mountains. Cadair Idris is almost as popular a climb as Snowdon. In Victorian times, and earlier, guides in Dolgellau accompanied visitors to the summit. The stone shelter was built to serve refreshments to walkers waiting for the mist to clear. You now have to take your own. The name Cadair Idris means Chair of Idris. The legendary Idris is said to have been a giant who lived on the mountain. It is said that anyone who spends a night on the mountain will wake up a poet or a madman.

4. Many years ago, people from the adjoining parishes of Talyllyn and Llanfihangel-y-Pennant used to meet at Carreg Enwau, on the Sabbath, for games and dances. One Easter Sunday, when a group of people were gathered, the Devil appeared on a slab of rock. He was in the body of an ass, and reared up on his hind legs as he let out a terrible howl, that made the surrounding mountains tremble. Everybody fled, and no one came to this spot for months afterwards. Eventually two local shepherds, one from Pencoed and the other from Rhiwogof, examined the rock and found the Devil's hoofprint. It became the custom for local shepherds to carve their names, with the date on the rock, hence the name, Carreg Enwau. The oldest name found is 1564. The stone is partly buried now. Mary Jones (see Walks 2 and 4) passed this way to Bala in 1800 when she walked barefoot from Llanfihangel to buy a Bible.

5. Popular with fishermen, the lovely Talyllyn Lake is named after the small settlement near it, the original name being Llyn Myngul. Opposite the Pen y Bont Hotel, St Mary's church is very ancient. Inside there is an arch of painted roses. An ornamental cross in the graveyard marks the grave of Jenny Jones, who was at the Battle of Waterloo with her husband.

Walk Directions: (-) denotes Point of Interest

1. Leave the Dôl Idris car park (1) by the signposted path behind the toilets, and go through a kissing-gate. Turn right, and follow the track when it veers left to another kissing-gate.

2. Continue on the track to a footbridge, and immediately turn right through a gate. Keep to the stepped path as you climb steeply through oak woodland.

3. Go through a gate in a wall on to open land. Continue on the main path with the stream below on the right. The path bears left gently into Cwm Cau.

4. When a huge cairn is met on the path, take the left fork. (The right path goes to Llyn Cau.) The path is steeper now, but you are soon rewarded with a fine view of Llyn Cau (2).

5. The path is marked by cairns as it bears to the right along the ridge. Keep climbing, and cross the ladder stile on Craig Cau.

6. Keep slightly left to avoid the cliff edge. The path descends to Bwlch Cau with its stone shoot. The final ascent takes a zigzag route to the cairn on the summit of Cadair Idris (3).

7. Take the path by which you arrived at the summit but in a few metres, when you reach a fork, keep to the right.

8. Take care not to go too close to the cliff edge. The path, well marked by cairns, passes along the cliffs above Llyn y Gadair. The route continues as a rough path and 2.5km from the summit, at fences, you will reach the Pony Path from Llanfihangel-y-Pennant to Ty-Nant. Here you leave the main path (which veers to the right, north).

9. Cross the ladder stile by the gate, and descend above a stream to a stile. Continue on a clear green path with marker posts to guide you. Cross a ladder stile and go downhill to a track. Keep left, descending to cross a stream and reach the sheep pens at Hafoty.

10. Go left over a ladder stile and follow the track. Cross another stile at a gate. In 50 metres bear left on a footpath, and follow a wall on the left. The path eventually veers away from the wall and reaches a ladder stile. Descend to a stream and cross an old stone footbridge.

11. Continue beside a fence on the left to reach a track and turn left. Go through gates, and in 300 metres turn left over a ladder stile. Descend the field to cross a footbridge. Keep ahead uphill, slightly left, to a ladder stile beside a gate.

12. Turn left on the track uphill. Cross a bridge and follow the track as it bends to the right. At the next bend turn right on a path, and go uphill to a gate gap in the wall.

13. Keep ahead through the field, and pass a stretch of broken wall on the left. Go through a gate and turn right to a ladder stile. The buildings of Pencoed are on your left.

14. Cross the field to a ladder stile above a ruin. Follow a wall on the right, and after it ends and continues as a fence, cross a stile in it. Descend to a ladder stile, and keep walking ahead through the valley.

15. Below a rock on your left, in about 300 metres, lies the flat stone known as Carreg Enwau (4). Cross a stream near a sheepfold, and continue ahead past a ruin on your left to join a track.

16. Turn right, and in 300 metres cross a stile at a gate. Continue on the track and cross a number of stiles, soon with good views of Talyllyn Lake (5). Bear right with the track towards Rhiwogof farm, and after crossing the stile just before it, turn left to have a fence on your left.

17. Go through a gate, and keep ahead on the green track. When it reaches a fence in a valley, you bear right to descend with the fence on your left. Go through a gate in the fence, cross a footbridge over a stream, and go through another gate. Pass a house, and continue on a green track to a lane.

18. Turn left through a gate and follow the lane, crossing a footbridge at a ford, to reach the B4405. Keep ahead to the car park near Minffordd.

Facilities:

Toilets in the car park. Cross Foxes Inn at the junction of the A487 and A470. Pubs at Talyllyn. Campsites nearby. Full facilities in Dolgellau.

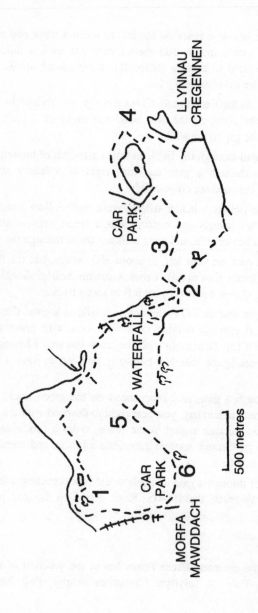

LLYNNAU
CREGENNEN

CAR
PARK

4

3

2

WATERFALL

5

6

CAR
PARK

1

500 metres

MORFA
MAWDDACH

42

Morfa Mawddach – Arthog Waterfalls – Llynnau Cregennen – Mawddach Trail – Morfa Mawddach

OS Maps:	1:50 000 Landranger Sheet 124; 1:25 000 Outdoor Leisure Sheet 23.
Start:	Car park near Morfa Mawddach station, G.R. 629141.
Access:	Leave the A493 about 1 mile north of Fairbourne on a lane signposted Morfa Mawddach station. The station is on the Cambrian Coast line. Bus stop at the lane end on the A493, Tywyn-Dolgellau bus route.
Parking:	Car park near Morfa Mawddach station.
Grade:	Moderate – estuary and disused railway tracks, woodland and lakeside paths, lane.
Time:	About 4½ hours.

Points of Interest:

1. The Mawddach estuary must be one of the loveliest in Europe. High on the moors above Llyn Tegid (Bala Lake) the Afon Mawddach starts its journey, trickling through the boggy Waun y Griafolen before tumbling into Coed y Brenin and over the Mawddach Falls. Several tributary rivers join the Mawddach before it reaches the sea – the Cain, Eden and Gamlan near Ganllwyd, the Wnion at Dolgellau, and many other small rivers. The path along the viaduct to Barmouth offers splendid views of the estuary.

2. The two enclosures of Llys Bradwen are about 25 metres to the right of the path. Stone covered banks, partly covered with heather, are the only remains of this medieval site. On flat ground, the larger enclosure may be 30 metres square. The other one is above it, and near a fence. The site may have been the court of a chieftain. According to local tradition, a law court was held here in the early 12th century.

3. The Bronze Age Arthog Circle is on private land, but can be seen over the wall. Only four stones remain in the circle, another two are on the outside, and there is a large quartz boulder. Other stones may have been used to build field walls.

4. Llynnau Cregennen were both given to the National Trust in 1959 by Major Wynne-Jones, in memory of his two sons who were both killed in the Second World War. Pared-y-cefn hir, a high steep hill behind the beautiful lakes, has a hill-fort along its ridge.

5. The Mawddach Trail starts in Barmouth and continues along the trackbed of the disused railway line, between Morfa Mawddach and Dolgellau. From Dolgellau, the former railway continued through Bala to Ruabon. Two sections of the line have been reopened for steam trains: one at Bala (along the side of Llyn Tegid) and the other at Llangollen. Ruabon to Barmouth was a fifty-four mile trip – a three hour journey with thirty-one passenger stops. The line was opened in the 1860s, linking the north-west of England with the Cambrian Coast line. Slate and copper from local quarries were transported on the line as freight. Sadly, lack of profits forced the closure of the line in 1965. Nowadays, the track is rich in wildlife. Flowers such as bird's foot trefoil, rest-harrow and purple loosestrife grow alongside the track.

6. Arthog Bog is a Site of Special Scientific Interest. Look and listen for reed bunting and curlew. A path leads into the RSPB reserve, and passes through willow and alder scrub to reach an attractive area of grassland. Warblers are here in the summer, and both marsh cinquefoil and heath spotted orchid may be seen in the meadow. Before the time of the railway, peat was cut in Arthog Bog, and taken by boat to Dolgellau and Barmouth.

Walk Directions: (-) denotes Point of Interest

1. From the car park near Morfa Mawddach station, walk in the direction of Barmouth and continue on the footpath beside the railway line. At a footpath signpost on the right, leave the path to follow an embankment to a barrier below the hill, Fegla Fawr.

2. Turn left on a track to have the hillside on your right. Just before the

Afon Mawddach (1) bear right, above the river, to some houses. Turn right, and soon follow a track behind the back gardens.

3. At the end of the houses, turn left to return to the Mawddach. Continue behind a small beach and, before a cattle grid, turn right through a gate. Bear left through another gate and follow the path beside a fence. At some trees leave the fence on a clear path, soon passing below a hill. Continue through open ground to reach a fence on the left. Follow it to a track.

4. Keep ahead and, opposite the track to Tyddyn Uchaf, turn right on a path between ditches. In 100 metres bear left through gorse, cross a small bridge, and continue to a track. Turn right, go through a gate, and cross the Mawddach Trail. In another 150 metres, turn left over a stile.

5. Pass a pool and follow a stream on your left. Continue to the A493. Turn left and, in a few metres, turn right to go up steps to a gate, signposted Arthog Waterfalls.

6. Follow the path uphill with a stream below on the left. In about 200 metres, a track joins from the right. Keep ahead, passing a wall and arrows on the left, and in another 30 metres turn right on a narrow path that climbs through rhododendrons.

7. In 200 metres, the waterfalls are on the left. Continue on the winding path and cross a ladder stile into a field. Veer to the left following the path close to the stream. Cross a few stiles and reach a grassy track.

8. Turn left, and quickly left again over a clapper bridge. To the right is the site of Llys Bradwen (2). Reach a grassy track and bear left to a gate. Ignore a track to the left and keep walking ahead until you emerge in a field.

9. Turn right to follow a wall. Go through a gate in a fence, and another in a wall. The Arthog Circle is in the field on the right (3). Keep walking ahead, then bear left on a walled track. Go through a gate, and turn left beside a wall that leads to a stone stile. Take a left-hand path to reach the lane at Llynnau Cregennen (4).

10. Turn left and pass the National Trust car park. Stay on the lane for

another 200 metres, then leave it at a marker post near a fence. Bear right to a ladder stile in a wall.

11. The path passes above the lake before veering away from it. At a National Trust post, turn right through heather to the lakeside. Continue with the lake on your right, and cross a ladder stile. Bear left to reach another lake and keep it on your left. Cross a ladder stile and keep walking ahead to the lane. About 80 metres to the right, there is a standing stone.

12. Go left through a gate and follow the lane to a junction. Turn right, passing a ruined farmhouse, and ignore a track on the left marked unsuitable for motor vehicles. In another 120 metres, turn right on a grassy track.

13. Go through a gate, follow a wall on the left, and pass through a wall gap. Continue with a wall on your right. After another gate, pass a house, and follow a fence down to the stream and the clapper bridge crossed earlier during the walk.

14. Ignore the ladder stile and continue through a gate to a lane. Turn right, pass a house on the right, and keep ahead. Before a right bend in the lane, turn left on a track through a gate. Follow a fence on the right, ignore a gate to a house on the left, and continue on the track to a gate on the right leading to a house called Merddyn.

15. Go through the gate, continue past the house, and follow a walled path through another gate. Keep ahead on the path, which becomes quite rough, zigzagging downhill through gorse, bracken and a couple of gates. Ignore the gates to the right.

16. Emerge on a lane and turn right to the A493. Bear right and in 200 metres, turn left at a footpath signpost on to a track. Go through a gate and keep ahead to the Mawddach Trail (5). Turn left, and follow the track past Arthog Bog (6) to the starting point.

Facilities:

Alternative parking at Llynnau Cregennen. Toilets in both car parks. Full facilities in Barmouth across the bridge (toll). Refreshments and narrow gauge railway in Fairbourne.

Barmouth (Y Bermo) – Bwlch y Llan – Panorama Walk – Dinas Olau – Barmouth (Y Bermo)

OS Maps:	1:50 000 Landranger Sheet 124; 1:25 000 Outdoor Leisure Sheet 23.
Start:	Near the railway station, Barmouth. G.R. 612158.
Access:	Barmouth is on the A496, 10 miles west of Dolgellau. Barmouth is on the Cambrian Coast line. Buses from Wrexham, Dolgellau and Blaenau Ffestiniog.
Parking:	Car parks signposted from the A496 in Barmouth.
Grade:	Moderate – hill paths.
Time:	3-4 hours.

Points of Interest:

1. Barmouth (Y Bermo) is a charming small resort situated below craggy hills at the mouth of the Mawddach. The Victorians discovered the town's attractions in 1867, when the first trains crossed the viaduct, and today the long sandy beach is still popular with families. Before the building of the railway Barmouth was a busy port, and much ship building took place in yards along the Mawddach. The medieval building near the harbour, Ty-gwyn, is where Jasper Tudor, the Earl of Pembroke, plotted with his supporters to overthrow Richard III and put the future Henry VI on the throne. Ty-crwn, the circular building also near the harbour, was built in the early 19th century to lock up drunks. Nowadays, the harbour is mainly used by pleasure craft. Barmouth is the starting point for the annual Three Peaks Yacht Race. This voyage to Fort William takes place in June, and requires the ascent of Snowdon, Scafell Pike and Ben Nevis, as well as sailing 350 miles.

2. The Victorian church of St John is beautiful and spacious. In 1887

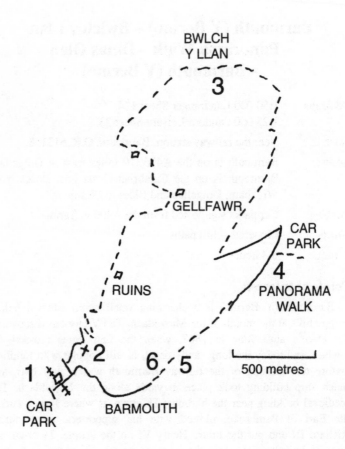

BWLCH
Y LLAN

3

GELLFAWR

CAR
PARK

4

PANORAMA
WALK

RUINS

1
CAR
PARK

2

6

5

500 metres

BARMOUTH

Princess Beatrice, daughter of Queen Victoria, laid the foundation stone for this ecclesiastical building, which is built of red sandstone brought in by rail from Chester. The Angel-font is made from white marble that was quarried in Italy.

3. A tragic accident occurred in Bwlch y Llan on Boxing Day, 1943. An Avro Anson flew into the hillside in low cloud, whilst returning to base at RAF Llandwrog after a routine navigational exercise. None of the four members of the crew survived.

4. To reach the Panorama Walk, follow the track – an old road to Barmouth – and go through a gate. Immediately go through another one on the right and keep walking ahead, bearing slightly left, to reach the summit. From here, almost the entire Mawddach estuary is visible. Fairbourne and its miniature railway is to the right along the coast, and to the left lies the magnificent Cadair Idris range. On a very clear day, looking up-river, it might be possible to see the Aran mountains. Below in the estuary, trains may be seen crossing Barmouth Bridge. The bridge has a swing section, and it featured in the film 'The Ghost Train' when a train fell into the sea. To build the bridge, 500 timber piles were driven into the sand. In 1981, some had to be replaced because they were being attacked by marine boring worms.

5. The Frenchman, Auguste Guyard, occupied one of the St George cottages in Barmouth. Guyard, an educationalist, had tried unsuccessfully to set up a community in his own village in France. Later, whilst staying in Paris, his friends included Alexander Dumas and Victor Hugo. At the time of the Franco-German War, Guyard fled from Paris and came to Wales, where he met the philanthropist, Mrs Fanny Talbot. She had given several cottages to her friend, the writer and socialist John Ruskin, who had set up the Guild of St George. He believed that the perfect life was living away from cities, working hard, and 'education of heart and mind'. Guyard became one of the tenants, and taught his neighbours how to cultivate and grow vegetables and herbs. He died in 1883.

6. The National Trust's first property was this 2 hectare piece of land called Dinas Olau. It was given by Mrs Talbot in March 1898. She lived nearby at Tynyffynnon. A stone seat commemorates the 100th

anniversary of the National Trust being given this headland. Views across Cardigan Bay stretch from Llyn to Pembrokeshire. Below, built on ledges against the rock, are the old houses of Barmouth, known as Gibraltar.

Walk Directions: (-) denotes Point of Interest

1. From the railway crossing, near the station in Barmouth (1), pass Jubilee Road on the right and walk towards the A496. Turn left past the traffic lights and bear right up St John's Hill. The road swings right, and just before the church (2), bear left up Gellfechan Road.

2. After a short climb there is a footpath signpost on the left, pointing right. Turn right, and pass the entrance of a house. Go uphill to a wider track. Turn right, and pass above the church. Go through a small gate on to another track and turn left, uphill, past the tunnels of manganese mines.

3. The track swings right. Continue, and where a green track keeps ahead, bear left on the clearer track so that the wall is on your left. Go uphill, through a gate, and pass a ruined barn on the left to go directly uphill. (The track takes a longer route to pass a ruined farmhouse.) Cross the track further up the hill, and follow a wall on the left.

4. Descend by the wall, and bear right at a wall gap on the left. A stream is now on the left. Go through a gate in a wall, and in about 50 metres, turn left over the stream and go through a small gate. Follow a fence on the right, and bear right with it past a ruined barn.

5. Before reaching a house, Gell-fawr, turn left uphill and pass another barn on the right. Continue uphill, soon with a wall on the left and gorse on the right. Bear left on a grassy track to pass above an old barn.

6. Continue to a ladder stile. Follow the green track to a marker post, and bear left to a ladder stile at a gate.

7. Go uphill to another green track. Turn right following a wall, nearby on the right, through Bwlch y Llan (3). The track descends to a level marshy area and bears left, away from the wall. About 100 metres from the wall, turn right uphill to a kissing-gate.

8. Descend a green path towards a mast. Follow a wall on the left, but before a stile and the mast, turn right to have a wall on the left. Cross a ladder stile and bear left. Shortly before a wall corner, the path bears right through a gap.

9. Contour the hillside, and at a marker post, continue beside a wall. Go through a wall gap, and follow the path to the left. In about 50 metres the path bears slightly right and descends, passing marker posts. Eventually, the path makes a right turn, and then descends to a gate at a lane.

10. Turn left on the lane and descend to another lane at a parking area. Turn right, and 50 metres beyond the car park, a gate gives access to the Panorama Walk (4).

11. Continue on the lane, downhill. In about 400 metres, at a footpath signpost on the right, follow a track uphill and, before a gate, turn right up steps. Turn left and pass a house on the left. The path bears left and goes through a gate.

12. Pass houses on the left, and at a track junction, bear right and go through a gate at a barn. Keep ahead on the track, and follow a fence on the left to a small gate. Take the clear path uphill and join a wall at a seat. In 250 metres, a gate on the left gives access to the Frenchman's Grave (5).

13. In another 80 metres, go through a gate on to Dinas Olau (6) and bear right to a viewpoint seat. Or, go directly downhill through gorse to a lane.

14. Turn right and descend to a lane junction. Keep right, and follow this lane as it bends left to the main road. Straight ahead is the level crossing and the starting place near the station and car parks.

Facilities:

Alternative car park (and portaloo) near the start of the Panorama Walk. Public toilets near the start. Full facilities in Barmouth, including a campsite.

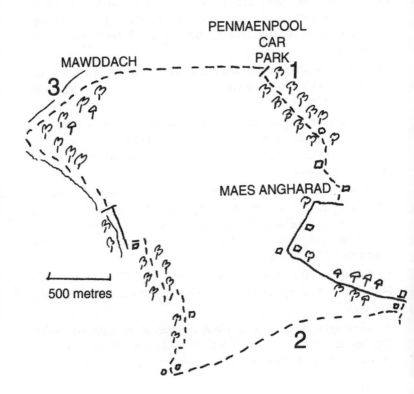

PENMAENPOOL
CAR
PARK

MAWDDACH

MAES ANGHARAD

500 metres

1

2

3

52

Penmaenpool (Pwll Penmaen) – Maes Angharad – Gellilwyd Farm – Pont Abergwynant – Penmaenpool (Pwll Penmaen)

OS Maps:	1:50 000 Landranger Sheet 124; 1:25 000 Outdoor Leisure Sheet 23.
Start:	Car park near the toll bridge at Penmaenpool. G.R. 695185.
Access:	Penmaenpool is on the A493, two miles west of Dolgellau. Buses from Dolgellau and Tywyn.
Parking:	Penmaenpool car park.
Grade:	Moderate – forest, moorland, fields, lane and estuary track bed of old railway.
Time:	3½-4 hours.

Points of Interest:

1. The George III Hotel in Penmaenpool (Pwll Penmaen) was built in 1650, and was originally two buildings: an inn, and a ship chandlers. The whole area was a centre for boat building, with many of the inlets along the Mawddach having boatyards, making sloops of oak from the local woodlands. All this activity ceased with the coming of the railways in the mid 19th century. The line only operated for about 100 years before closing in 1965. The old signal box is an RSPB centre. Lapwings, shelduck, common sandpiper, red-breasted merganser, curlew, heron and cormorants may be spotted with the binoculars, available for public use, at the centre. The nearby toll bridge, over the head of the Mawddach, was built in 1879 and could be opened for the passage of ships. Gerard Manley Hopkins stayed at the George III Hotel and wrote a poem about Penmaenpool: 'O where live well your lease of leisure But here at, here at Penmaenpool'.

2. This walled track was almost certainly a drovers' route. A hill on the left rises to about 900ft. At the western end of the hill, Craig y Castell on the map, sprawl the broken ramparts of an Iron Age hill-fort.

3. The Mawddach Trail is a 9 mile footpath from Barmouth to Dolgellau. From Morfa Mawddach it follows the track bed of the Ruabon-Barmouth railway line, which opened in the 1860s bringing Victorians from north-west England to the Cambrian Coast and taking slate and copper in the other direction. On the northern side of the estuary runs the Meirionnydd gold belt – Clogau (see Walk 9) above Y Bont-ddu was one of the richest mines.

Walk Directions: (-) denotes Point of Interest

1. From the car park at Penmaenpool (1), walk up to the A493 and turn right in the direction of Tywyn. In 50 metres, turn left at a footpath signpost. Follow the path to a lane and turn left.

2. On reaching a fork, turn right on a rough track that climbs steadily through woodland. At a small pool on the left, look on the right for a yellow arrow and a narrow path. Follow it to a ladder stile.

3. Keep ahead to a track, and bear right. When the track divides, take the left fork (ahead) and go through a gate. Keep a cottage on the left but, before the end of the cottage, turn left across grass to a waymark and a fence type stile.

4. Bear right and descend the field, passing a telegraph pole and a wooded hillock on your right. Go through a gap in the wall ahead, and continue through a broad gate. Take the path uphill and at a fence turn right then left above a farmhouse, Maes Angharad. Go over a ladder stile, and cross the field to the next stile and a lane.

5. Turn right on the lane. In about 200 metres, it goes through a gate and then bears left. Continue on the lane past Tal-y-Waen and through woods to Gellilwyd Fawr, passing it on your left. In another 30 metres turn right to cross a ladder stile, and pass a barn.

6. Do not follow the obvious track ahead. Instead, bear right on a green track uphill, with a wall nearby on the right. Go through a gate

so that you have a coniferous plantation on the right. The track bears left away from the trees, and to the left of a mound, to reach a stile and gate at a walled track.

7. This ancient walled track (2) crosses the moorland for about a mile. At the end it may be blocked for a few metres, but it is easy enough to walk beside it. Go through a gate, pass a barn on the right and follow a wall on the left.

8. Keep ahead and descend a track through woodland. Reach a level track and turn right. Go through a gate and bear left. Almost immediately, turn right past a building to a gate. Keep ahead and in 100 metres bear right, uphill, on a green track.

9. Reach a stream and a wood on the left. About 20 metres before a gate, bear right on a narrow path to a footbridge. Cross a wall on the left and head towards a broken wall. Turn right before it, and go through the wall gap ahead. Take a winding path uphill.

10. At a wall go through a gate, and continue to some houses. Keep the houses on the right to follow a track downhill through open fields, and through a gate into woodland. From the next gate continue to where the track bears left, then leave the track to keep ahead across stone slabs over a stream. Turn left and cross the second stile on the right.

11. Pass above buildings, and descend the field slanting past trees to a stone stile, about 50 metres from the far field corner, above a house. Turn left on a track, and follow it to a lane. Turn right to the A493.

12. Cross the road and bear left a few metres. Turn right on a track to Abergwynant Farm. Continue with the river on the left, but where the lane crosses the river, keep walking ahead on a track and through a gate.

13. Continue beside the river and through another gate, soon entering woods. Turn left and follow the track to an open area. Ignore the track to the right but keep ahead through a gate on to the old railway track, alongside Afon Mawddach (3).

14. Turn right and follow the disused railway track, the Mawddach Trail (3), for about 3km to the starting point at Penmaenpool.

Facilities:

Public toilets near the car park. Refreshments in summer at the George III Hotel. RSPB Centre. All facilities in Dolgellau.

Bont-ddu – Coed Garth-gell
– Afon Cwm-mynach – Hirgwm
– Afon Mawddach – Bont-ddu

OS Maps:	1:50 000 Landranger Sheet 124; 1:25 000 Outdoor Leisure Sheet 23.
Start:	Car park at the Fiddler's Elbow, east of Bont-ddu. G.R. 678189.
Access:	Bont-ddu is on the A496, 7km west of Dolgellau. Buses from Barmouth, Dolgellau and Wrexham.
Parking:	Snowdonia National Park car park at the Fiddler's Elbow, 800m east of Bont-ddu.
Grade:	Moderate – woodland, hill and estuary paths.
Time:	3-3½ hours.

Points of Interest:

1. Coed Garth-gell is a beautiful sessile oak wood belonging to the RSPB, as part of their Mawddach Reserve. Here, in summer, you may see pied flycatchers, warblers, redstart and tree pipits. The hillsides along the Mawddach were once covered with deciduous trees, but these were felled for house and ship building, and the oak bark used for tanning.

2. The Garth-gell gold mine opened in the 1860s, and was worked intermittently by different owners until it was abandoned in 1903. The only recorded output is for 1901, when 5oz of gold was produced from 26 tons of ore. The round structures on the mill site are buddles, which were used for separating the ore. Look out for grey wagtails and dipper along Afon Cwm-mynach.

3. Originally worked for copper, the Clogau mine became the richest producer of gold in Meirionnydd. The discovery of the precious metal

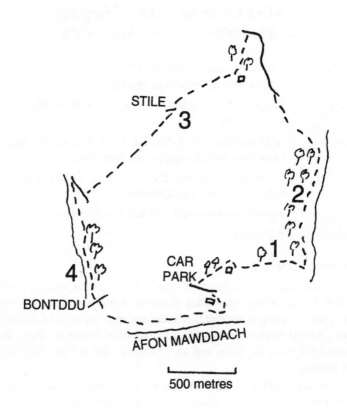

STILE

3

2

CAR
PARK

1

4

BONTDDU

ÁFON MAWDDACH

500 metres

was made by chance in February 1854, when the proprietors were examining the lodes. One of the partners broke a piece of quartz taken from a dump and found it contained gold. The following day, villagers helped to search for the gold quartz and they collected nearly a ton of ore. Crushing and amalgamating machines were installed at the Figra mill, but these were inefficient and extracted very little gold. The company became bankrupt, and the new Figra and Clogau Copper Mining Company started operating for copper in the old Clogau mine in 1858. The search for gold continued, and within two years, it was struck in the St David's Lode. By the end of June 1862 the output was 320oz a fortnight. This high grade ore was soon exhausted, and it became necessary to crush a greater quantity of quartz to extract any gold. To increase efficiency, a system of tramways replaced the horses and carts that used to take the ore down Clogau. In spite of new machinery, little gold was extracted and a succession of companies followed. A much deeper adit, called the Tyncornel Adit, was driven through to the St David's Lode. Gold was recognised, but it took yet another company's investment to extend the adit. The company withdrew, and in 1891 some local men invested in the mine with successful results. By 1894 it was estimated their profit was £10,000. From 1894 bigger companies took over, employing over 100 men. In the year 1904, 18,417 ounces of gold was extracted, but this was followed by a gradual slackening in production until the mine ceased operations in 1911. Since then, some small companies have, at various times, worked the mine.

4. The Figra crushing mill, located beside Hirgwm, was driven by a huge 12 metre waterwheel. Berdan and Britten pans were used for grinding the ore. Developed for use in California, the Berdan pan was a revolving bowl containing two balls of different sizes. The popular Britten pan was favoured for more valuable ore.

Walk Directions: (-) denotes Point of Interest

1. From the parking place, take the track beside the footpath signpost. It climbs to a wall on the left. In another 120 metres go through a small gate in the wall, and bear right to follow a path until you reach another gate.

2. Rejoin the track and continue uphill. The track bears right and descends towards a house. Go through a gate, and take a path on the left side of the building. Go under an arch and turn left across grass to emerge on a path with wonderful views of the Mawddach.

3. Follow the path to a stile and descend through trees to another stile. Continue on a rough path and follow a broken moss covered wall. Reach an RSPB reserve sign (1).

4. Continue past ruins, following arrows. The path broadens and descends steeply to another track. Bear right to an RSPB information board.

5. Bear left to go through a gate, and continue on an old track with Afon Cwm-mynach tumbling below. In 800m, a path to the right leads to the buddles of a gold mine (2).

6. Continue on the track, and pass the smithy ruins on the left. At the end of the reserve cross a ladder stile.

7. Continue on a clear path which bends to the left. Keep ahead and go through a gate. Descend to the right past a building, and continue to a gate and a bridge.

8. Turn left on the lane. Cross an old stone bridge over the river, and in another 150 metres go left to a ladder stile. Follow the obvious path slanting left towards woodland. In 200 metres, cross stone steps in a wall on the left.

9. Keep ahead and follow a path and arrows uphill through trees. Reach a track and turn right to the building called Garth-gell. At a track junction, fork right uphill to a wall. Continue in the same direction on a narrow path, marked by a few blobs or arrows of yellow paint.

10. Reach a wall corner, and ignore a stone stile. Continue with the wall on your left, and after a wet area, cross a ladder stile on the left. A spoil heap of the Clogau gold mine is nearby (3).

11. Turn right and pass through a gate to follow a green track. Go through another gate and continue on a clear path. Reach an arrow and bear right to follow its direction across the hillside.

12. With a wall nearby on the left, go through a gate to follow a wall and later a fence on your right. At a gate ahead, bear right between a wall and fence to a lane. Turn right past a house.

13. Just before the lane crosses a bridge, turn left through a kissing-gate and follow a path above the river. Go through a wall gap, and later a gate, to join an enclosed track. Reach another track and bear left. To the right is the Llechfraith Adit, a Clogau mine.

14. Continue with the river on your right. At some houses, continue beside the river and ignore a bridge, site of the Figra mill (4). Go through a kissing-gate and through woodland to another gate and descend to a path above afon Hirgwm. In 200 metres the path bears left and goes through a gate, near a house.

15. Descend steps past houses, and bear left in front of a house to a lane parallel to the A496. Turn left, and in 80 metres turn right at a footpath signpost and track.

16. In 120 metres, keep ahead on a path to rejoin the track again. Go through a gate, pass buildings on the left and continue through gorse to a kissing-gate.

17. Follow the path alongside woodland, and later a field. Go up steps and bear right on an embankment. Turn left above the Mawddach and continue to a kissing-gate.

18. Bear right to follow an arrow. Go through a gate and in a few paces, turn left to another gate. Pass in front of Rhuddallt, and follow the drive to the A496. Turn left to the starting point.

Facilities:

Picnic tables at the car park. Refreshments at Bont-ddu and Dolgellau. Full facilities in Dolgellau.

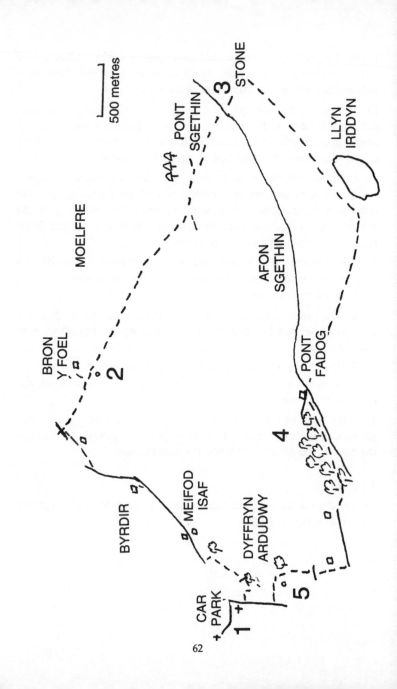

62

Dyffryn Ardudwy – Bryn-y-foel – Pont Sgethin – Pontfadog – Coed Corsygedol – Dyffryn Ardudwy

OS Maps:	1:50 000 Landranger Sheet 124; 1:25 000 Outdoor Leisure Sheet 18.
Start:	Car park, Dyffryn Ardudwy, G.R. 586232.
Access:	Dyffryn Ardudwy is on the A496, north of Barmouth. Railway station on the Cambrian Coast line less than 800m. Dyffryn Ardudwy is on the Barmouth-Harlech bus route.
Parking:	Station Road, Dyffryn Ardudwy.
Grade:	Moderate – field, moorland and woodland paths, lane.
Time:	About 5 hours.

Points of Interest:

1. Llanenddwyn church can be found by following the road to the right for just over 400m. It is a 16th century cruciform church, and has the original roofs and font. In the porch there are early 19th century notices about feeding the poor, and the churchyard contains several 200 year old gravestones.

2. The Bron-y-foel Isaf Neolithic burial chamber was probably a portal dolmen. These tombs had tall entrance stones and large capstones. This 5000 year old monument has a three metre capstone but most of the other stones have gone.

3. The bridge, Pont Sgethin, was built to carry the London to Harlech mail coach across Afon Sgethin. Cattle droves, starting in Llanbedr, also came this way on their journey to England. From the early Middle Ages, until after the coming of the railways, thousands of cattle from North and Mid Wales were driven hundreds of miles to English

markets. Cattle were shod for the journey, and on their cloven hoofs they wore two arcs of narrow metal. Droves could be half a mile or more long, and small dogs were used to keep the cattle together. They started at dawn and usually covered two miles an hour. The dangers included wolves and robbers, and people wanting to journey to England often joined the drovers for safety. By Elizabethan times drovers had to have a licence, and to apply for one, a man needed to be over thirty years of age, be a householder and married. In Victorian times, droves could not take place on Sundays.

4. To visit the Cors-y-gedol Neolithic burial chamber, continue on the lane for about 400 metres. It is on the left, quite close to the lane. Most of the stones have gone, and the tomb has only two upright stones and a large capstone. Originally, it would have been enclosed in a rectangular cairn. Another name for the monument is Arthur's Quoit. King Arthur is said to have thrown the largest stone, the capstone, from the top of Moelfre. Some indentations on the stone are claimed to be the marks of his fingers.

5. The Dyffryn Ardudwy Neolithic burial cairn consists of two chambers, both facing up the hill. The lower, smaller tomb is a fine example of a portal dolmen – tall entrance stones fronting a rectangular chamber, topped with a sloping capstone. Excavation took place in 1960, and in front of both structures there were offerings of broken pottery. The larger chamber was built later and contained Bronze Age cremated bones. The earlier tomb had its own small cairn, but when the second chamber was made a huge rectangular cairn – about 125 foot long by 55 foot wide – was built to enclose both tombs.

Walk Directions: (-) denotes Point of Interest

1. From Dyffryn Ardudwy car park, walk out to Station Road (1) and bear left to the A496. Turn right and in 150 metres, just after passing a chapel on the right, go left on a wide footpath. It passes between gardens.

2. The path bends to the right and goes through a kissing-gate on the left. Follow the path uphill into trees. Continue beside a wall on the left, and reach a lane.

3. Turn left and, in a few paces, bear right through a small gate at a footpath signpost. Follow the wall on the left, go through a wall gap and continue uphill towards trees. At the top wall, turn left through a gap and keep walking ahead. Descend the field slanting left to a small gate and lane.

4. Turn right to follow the gated lane. Pass Meifod Isaf, and in another 800m ignore the lane to Byrdir on the left. Pass farm buildings, and descend to a valley and stream. A few paces beyond a gate, turn right to take a narrow path uphill.

5. Go through a gate, and follow a left hand wall until it bends left. Keep ahead across the middle of the field, go through a wall gap and continue to a track. Bear right through the gate, follow the walled track and pass a house on the right. Enter a yard and veer left to a gate between buildings.

6. Continue beside a wall on the left and, shortly after it bears left, turn right through a small gate. Keep ahead with a wall on the left to a kissing-gate and lane.

7. Turn right on this access lane to Bron-y-foel. In 400 metres, before reaching a barn, turn right on a track. Go through a gate and, in about 25 metres, look for the remains of a burial chamber on the right (2).

8. Follow this ancient track below Moelfre until it joins another track in 2km. Turn left and you will shortly have coniferous trees above, on the left. (At the end of the trees stands the ruin of a coaching inn on the old London-Harlech road. The road took the pass between Moelfre and Moelyblithcwm.) About halfway along the plantation, turn right on a path.

9. The path descends to Pont Sgethin (3). Cross the bridge and follow the path to the right across some planks at a wet area. Bear left with the path and in 400 metres, at an upright stone on the left, turn right on a narrow path.

10. Stay on the main path, which is for most of the way an old drove-road. It goes through a number of gates and passes Llyn Irddyn in a little over 1km. In another 2.5km, it meets a descending wall and bears right to Pontfadog. A stone in the middle of the bridge bears the date

1762. (Turning left at the wall would have taken you to Bwlch y Rhiwgyr, the drove-road to the Mawddach valley and Dolgellau.)

11. Cross the bridge and follow the lane uphill to the cottage, Llety Lloegr. This used to be a stopping place for drovers and a shoeing station. A diversion can be made from here to see the Corsygedol burial chamber (4).

12. Opposite the cottage, take the path at the bridleway sign. Follow it through the woods and alongside Afon Sgethin. About 800m from the lane the path leaves the river, and in a further 200 metres passes a seat on the right. In a few paces, the path divides. Ignore the left descending path and take the right fork. In about 60 metres it reaches a track.

13. Turn right, and in 150 metres turn left on another track. At a junction, keep ahead with a fence on your right. Cross a plank bridge and go through a small gate in a wall.

14. Join an access lane and follow it for 500 metres. Before reaching houses, cross a stone stile on the right. Bear right to follow the left hand wall and in 50 metres, turn left through a small gate.

15. Keep ahead beside a wall on the left, continue up steps and through another gate to cross a wide wall. Descend steps into the field and turn right. Follow a short walled track through a gate. Leave the left wall, and bear right to join a track coming from a house.

16. Turn left on the track, continue past farm buildings and through gates to a lane. Cross to a gate. Slant right, uphill, in the field and follow a wall closely on the right. Cross the broken wall ahead, and continue alongside the wall and a wood to a corner stile.

17. Cross a stream and follow the path through the trees. Descend to a wall on the left. Keep ahead and, at a corner, enter a field. Slant half left, going between telegraph poles, to reach a small gate. Follow a wall on the left to a kissing-gate, giving access to burial chambers (5).

18. Continue on the path to the A496. Turn right to Station Road and the starting point.

Facilities:

Public toilets near the road junction in Dyffryn Ardudwy. Refreshments Dyffryn Ardudwy, Tal-y-bont and Llanbedr. Rural Life Museum at Tal-y-bont. Campsites nearby.

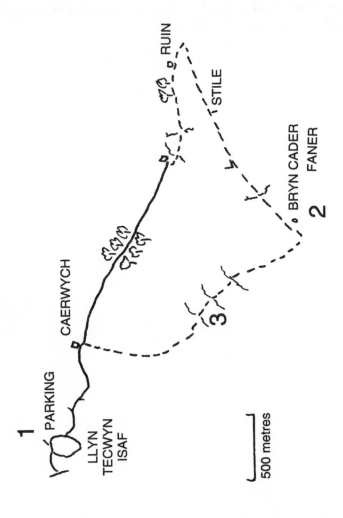

PARKING

LLYN
TECWYN
ISAF

CAERWYCH

RUIN

STILE

BRYN CADER
FANER

1

2

3

500 metres

68

Llyn Tecwyn Isaf – Coed Caerwych – Bryn Cader Faner – Llyn Tecwyn Isaf

OS Maps:	1:50 000 Landranger Sheet 124; 1:25 000 Outdoor Leisure Sheet 18.
Start:	Llyn Tecwyn Isaf, G.R. 630371.
Access:	North of Harlech, leave the A496 at Talsarnau. Take a minor road to Llandecwyn. In 2.5km, at a chapel, turn right to the lake. Alternatively, take the road uphill opposite the toll bridge road for Penrhyndeudraeth. Buses pass along the A496, about 1.5km from the start.
Parking:	At the lake or near Llandecwyn church.
Grade:	Moderate – lane and moorland paths.
Time:	About 3½ hours.

Points of Interest:

1. Llyn Tecwyn Isaf is a beautiful small lake, secluded in a hollow and almost surrounded by trees. Both white and yellow water lilies are prolific in summer, whilst little grebe and moorhen may be present. The lake is quite popular with fishermen.

2. Bryn Cader Faner is a small Bronze Age cairn with a circle of upright stones that lean outwards. Although the stones are only about one metre high, the design of this monument is dramatically effective in its isolated setting. It was probably a small cairn, rather than a ceremonial circle. The grave at the centre has been destroyed, and the army pulled out a few of the stones during manoeuvres between the 1st and 2nd World Wars.

3. To the left of the path, about 150 metres before crossing the stream below Y Gyrn, lies a Bronze Age burial cairn, recognizable by its hollowed centre with a ring of stones around it. About a further 80 metres along the path, look for a ring cairn on the opposite side of the stream.

Walk Directions: (-) denotes Point of Interest

1. From the parking area at Llyn Tecwyn Isaf (1) walk along the lane, passing the lake on your right. Go downhill through trees to a lane junction, and turn right.

2. The lane goes uphill and reaches a fork. Do not take the right hand lane (which goes over a cattle grid) but, instead, keep ahead through a gate.

3. Continue uphill on the lane, and go through another gate to pass the farmhouse of Caerwych on your left. Continue through gates and deciduous woodland, and beside a stream. In more open country, the lane passes a number of ruins.

4. At a house, Nant Pasgen Bach, turn right at a bridleway sign. Follow the path through wall gaps, and keep ahead to a ruin. Cross a stream.

5. Bear left on a walled path. Cross another stream, and continue on a path with a wall at varying distances on your left. Go through a wall gap, and follow a wall on the left and through some trees. There are more trees below, and the path turns left on a shelf above them.

6. In about 30 metres the path bears right and heads towards a ruin. From the ruin, continue with a wall on the right. Before reaching the corner of the wall, slant away from it uphill. Trawsfynydd Lake and Power Station come into view.

7. Veer to the right and pass the wall on your right. Keep ahead to an upper wall below crags, and go through a gap in the wall.

8. Turn right through heather and bracken, following the wall on your right. This is a Bronze Age track, which started at Llanbedr and finished south of Trawsfynydd. At varying distances along the route remain standing stones, cairns, mounds and, later hut settlements.

9. In about 500 metres the path leaves the wall to cross a stream. It then ascends to a wall again and soon crosses a ladder stile.

10. The wall bends right. Continue on a path above the wall, and head towards crags. When a fence beside the crags makes a sharp right bend, leave the crag to slant left (south-west) on a faint path across

moorland. After some damp ground, pass some outcrops on the right. Continue south-west and cross a stream. This point is about 400 metres from the crag.

11. About 20 metres beyond the stream, the path improves considerably. In another 300 metres, a path is seen approaching from hilly ground on the right. When the paths meet – or about 60 metres before this – turn left up the hill to Bryn Cader Faner (2).

12. Return to the path and turn right (west) through boggy ground, and follow the wide green path (seen earlier) uphill. Ignore paths leaving this main path. It descends past a hill on the left, and bears left over a stream. Keep left, passing a rocky hill on the right, and continue across damp ground. After crossing a stream, reach a firmer path.

13. About 150 metres after crossing the stream, two cairns may be located nearby. One is to the left of the path, and the other a little distance ahead on the opposite side of the water (3).

14. Continue on the path and cross the stream. Bear left under the rocky hill of Y Gyrn, and soon there are wonderful views of the Dwyryd estuary and the Llŷn peninsula.

15. Follow the main path through a gate on to a wide grassy path. After another gateway, look for some round huts alongside the path. Continue through gates, and eventually follow a wall on the left to reach the lane at Caerwych.

16. Turn left to pass Caerwych, and retrace your steps to the starting point at Llyn Tecwyn Isaf.

Facilities:

Refreshments at Talsarnau and Maentwrog. Camp sites nearby. Harlech Castle. Portmeirion.

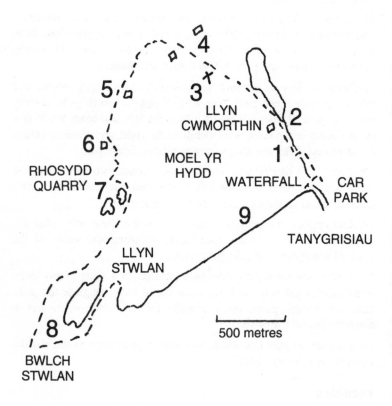

4

5

3

2

LLYN
CWMORTHIN

1

6

MOEL YR
HYDD

RHOSYDD
QUARRY

7

WATERFALL

CAR
PARK

9

TANYGRISIAU

LLYN
STWLAN

500 metres

8

BWLCH
STWLAN

Tanygrisiau – Llyn Cwmorthin – Bwlch Cwmorthin – Llyn Stwlan – Tanygrisiau

OS Maps: 1:50 000 Landranger Sheet 124, 115;
               1:25 000 Outdoor Leisure Sheet 18. 17.

Start: Parking area near the footbridge and waterfall below
               Cwmorthin, G.R. 682454.

Access: From the A487, 1.5km south of Blaenau Ffestiniog, take
               the road signed Ffestiniog Power Station. Pass the
               Visitor Centre and turn right over the Ffestiniog Railway
               level crossing. Bear right to cross a bridge, then left to
               the parking area. Trains and buses to Blaenau
               Ffestiniog. Local bus and narrow gauge railway to
               Tanygrisiau.

Parking: Parking at the waterfall below Cwmorthin.

Grade: Moderate – mainly rough paths and tracks.

Time: About 3½ hours.

Points of Interest:

1. Wrysgan quarry operated intermittently for over a hundred years from the 1830s. Slate was originally brought down to Cwmorthin by pack animals but later, a long incline connected the quarry directly with the Ffestiniog Railway. Remains include the ruined mill, reservoir, and the spectacular incline cut by the Llyn Stwlan access road. Roof falls have made the underground workings dangerous to enter.

2. The huge glacier that once filled Cwmorthin left behind a rock barrier, which formed a dam for the lake. Water lilies may be seen here in summer. Quarrymen lived in the nearby houses, and a little further to the left stand the walls of the ruined chapel. Other buildings belonging to the Cwmorthin Quarry can be seen on the northern shore

of the lake. This was a very big quarry, as shown by the huge tips, and 500 men were employed when output increased after the opening of the Ffestiniog Railway. A tramway connected the quarry with the railway at Tanygrisiau. Less slate was produced after a collapse in 1884, and later it became part of the Oakley quarry.

3. Before 1867, when the Rhosydd Chapel was built, there was no regular place for the quarrymen's children to attend school. The building was paid for by the men, not the quarry company, and on weekdays it served as a school. On Sundays religious meetings were held in the chapel, which has not been used since the 1920s.

4. The manager of the Rhosydd quarry lived at Plas Cwmorthin, the house sheltered by trees and now a ruin. Built in 1860, it had four rooms on each floor and a basement. Near the track is the Rhosydd stable, and further on, Rhosydd Terrace. Each of these six cottages was occupied by a quarryman and his wife and children. Above the track, part-way up the hillside, are the adits of the small Conglog quarry. Its incline descended to a mill near the terrace, and the finished slate was transported by tramway through Cwmorthin quarry. The stream plunging down the hillside is an outflow of Llyn Conglog, a lake which lies on lonely moorland high above this cwm. Before the quarrymen came, the track through Cwmorthin was a drovers' route for animals brought from Cwmorthin and Llanfrothen.

5. Bwlch Cwmorthin was floor 9 for the Rhosydd quarry, and here stood the main mill. The remains of two rows of barracks are to the left and behind them the main adit, which is over 600 metres long. Men lodged in the barracks from Monday to Saturday. They walked in from the villages of Beddgelert, Croesor, Llan Ffestiniog and further afield. However, the barracks were notorious for their lack of ventilation and overcrowded conditions. At first, the quarry had transport problems. Because only bridleway rights existed through Cwmorthin, Rhosydd had to transport the slate by pack animals. Cwmorthin quarry rarely allowed the use of carts. After plans for a Rhosydd Railway failed, C.E. Spooner designed a superb incline which descended to the Croesor Tramway. It started operating in 1864. From the mill on floor 9, a tramway ran for 800 metres to a shelf

cut into the mountain above Cwm Croesor. The impressive incline falls about 200 metres into the cwm, at a gradient of less than 1 in 2. The drum was above the track. Walk out to it if you have the time – follow the level track ahead – the views of Cwm Croesor and Y Cnicht are magnificent. After work on summer evenings, the Rhosydd choir would make a procession to the incline, their voices echoing around the head of the cwm.

6. Barracks, a smithy and a privy are on this level, floor 4. If you follow a grassy path along the tip on the right, you will be rewarded with fine views of Y Cnicht, Cwm Croesor and the Rhosydd remains on Bwlch Cwmorthin below.

7. These open pits (Twll y Dwyrain [East] and Twll y Gorllewin [West] are the top of Rhosydd quarry, and the earliest workings. Slate was first worked here on a small scale in the 1830s. After the transport problem was solved, Rhosydd developed into a large underground quarry with 14 levels, 170 chambers, and employed around 200 men. Rhosydd closed in 1930.

8. Llyn Stwlan was a small corrie lake until the arrival of the Ffestiniog Hydro-Electric pumped storage power station. Water, dropping 300 metres from the lake, turns the 360 megawatt turbines and at night, when the demand for electricity is low, water is pumped back to Llyn Stwlan by using electricity from the National Grid. The man-made Llyn Ystradau (Tanygrisiau reservoir) holds the water that falls from Stwlan.

9. Ffestiniog railway was first opened in 1836 for transporting slates from the quarries around Blaenau Ffestiniog to the quay at Porthmadog. The loaded trams descended to Porthmadog by gravity. Horses, that had ridden down, hauled the empty wagons uphill back to Blaenau Ffestiniog. Steam took over in 1863, one of the earliest locomotives being Prince. Later, larger locomotives were used and Myrddin Emrys was built in 1879 at Boston Lodge. After the slate traffic decreased and passenger services stopped during the 2nd World War, it was decided to close the line in 1946. Railway enthusiasts formed a rescue committee, and by 1957 the line was open again as far as Penrhyndeudraeth. But beyond Y Dduallt there was a problem. The

construction of Llyn Ystradau had lost the original tunnel and destroyed the track bed of the railway. A new tunnel was built higher up, and to reach this a spiral was engineered at Y Dduallt to gain the extra height. In 1983 the railway station in Blaenau Ffestiniog was officially opened, and trains once again run between here and Porthmadog.

Walk Directions: (-) denotes Point of Interest

1. From the parking area, take the track uphill and pass the waterfall on the left. At a level area, turn left through a gate into a 'garden'.

2. Go through another gate and continue on a path beside a pool. Ignore an old path on the left which goes up to the Wrysgan quarry (1).

3. The path climbs gently to the ruined houses at Llyn Cwmorthin (2). With the lake on your right, follow the level track through the cwm. Pass the isolated Rhosydd Chapel (3) on your left.

4. As you approach a gate you will see other ruins, including Plas Cwmorthin (4), in trees to your right. Take the old track slanting left, uphill.

5. At a level area, you will pass a large wheel-pit on the right. It was never used. Another short climb brings you to Bwlch Cwmorthin, and the main working area of Rhosydd quarry (5).

6. Turn left between ruined houses and a wheel-pit. Pass a tunnel on the left, and climb an incline to the remains of a drum house. Continue on the path, and up another incline, to a level area with a fine view of Y Cnicht on the right, and Moelwyn Mawr ahead (6).

7. Turn left at the drumhouse, and ascend between tips. Pass ruins on the right and reach another drumhouse. The mountain Moel yr Hydd is directly ahead.

8. Turn right, and in about 100 metres, take a path on the left to shortly pass pits on the right (7). The path bears to the right, and you will reach a small gate at a fence in the col, between Moel yr Hydd and Moelwyn Mawr.

9. Go through the gate and bear right. In a few paces, leave the fence to turn left on a path between outcrops. Follow this clear path along the south side of the mountain. Ahead is Moelwyn Bach.

10. Follow this fairly level, but stony, path below the rocky ridge of Craigysgafn. On a clear day views stretch to the Arenig and Rhinog mountains. Soon Llyn Stwlan lies below and the path continues over screes, passing grilled mine adits. It then rises gently to the col, Bwlch Stwlan, between Moelwyn Bach and Craigysgafn.

11. Turn left now, and aim for the end of Llyn Stwlan's Dam (8). Cross some boggy ground, and climb between outcrops to reach the far end of the wall.

12. Descend steps, and slant left to another wall. Where the wall breaks at a rock, climb to the opposite side and turn left to steps and a gate, leading on to the dam.

13. Cross the dam and follow the road. On the left, you will pass steps to a viewpoint. Continue down the zigzags with the incline of Moelwyn quarry, at first, on your right.

14. Llyn Ystradau lies below, and further on you will see the power station and possibly hear trains running along the narrow gauge Ffestiniog railway (9).

15. Pass the Wrysgan incline which descends from a tunnel high on the mountain and, in another 350 metres where the road bends right, turn left beside a fence. Cross a footbridge below the waterfall, and in a few paces you will reach the starting point at the car park.

Facilities:

Cafe and toilets at the Ffestiniog Visitor Centre. Myfanwy's licensed restaurant in Blaenau Ffestiniog. For tours of the Power Station, book at the Visitor Centre. Ffestiniog narrow gauge railway. Llechwedd Slate Caverns.

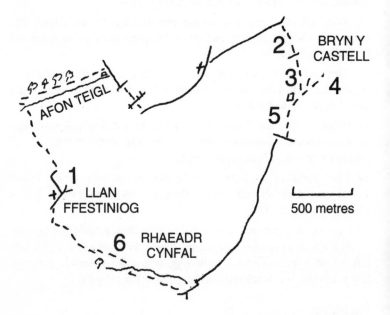

BRYN Y
CASTELL

2

3
4

5

AFON TEIGL

1
LLAN
FFESTINIOG

500 metres

6   RHAEADR
CYNFAL

78

Llan Ffestiniog – Coed Pengwern – Afon Teigl
– Hafod Ysbyty – Rhaeadr Cynfal
– Llan Ffestiniog

OS Maps:	1:50 000 Landranger Sheet 124;
	1:25 000 Outdoor Leisure Sheet 18.
Start:	Square near the Pengwern Arms, Llan Ffestiniog.
	G.R. 700419.
Access:	Llan Ffestiniog is on the A470, south of Blaenau Ffestiniog. Buses from Blaenau Ffestiniog, Dolgellau, Barmouth and Porthmadog.
Parking:	In the square at Llan Ffestiniog, also a small car park nearby.
Grade:	Moderate – field, woodland, lane and open country.
Time:	3½-4 hours.

Points of Interest:

1. The village of Llan Ffestiniog is located three miles from the slate quarrying town of Blaenau Ffestiniog. It stands above the lovely Vale of Ffestiniog, one of the beauty spots much visited by travellers taking the Celtic Grand Tour in the 18th and 19th centuries. Lord Lyttleton was enraptured by the Ffestiniog area – 'With the woman one loves, with the friend of one's heart, and a good study of books, one might pass an age here and think it a day'. A story in the Mabinogion tells how the wizard Gwydion created Blodeuwedd from flowers in the Vale of Ffestiniog. A path beside the church leads to a fine viewpoint of the vale.

2. Hafod Ysbyty was a stopping place for the bandits of Ysbyty Ifan on their raids of Dolwyddelan. They had taken over the hospice at Ysbyty Ifan when the order of the Knights of St John was abolished in the 14th century. The knights founded the hospice in AD1190 to give

food and shelter to travellers and they were given exemptions and immunity from law breaking, which meant that no Crown Officer could enter their property to arrest anyone. When the knights left, the immunity remained, and the hospice became a haven for outlaws. The fertile valley of Dolwyddelan was repeatedly raided until the Welsh chieftain Maredudd ap Ifan, with the co-operation of other local men, managed to drive them away.

3. Sarn Helen is a Roman Road linking the forts between Caerhun (near Conwy) and Caerfyrddin. Sarn means road, and according to a story in Y Mabinogion it was named after the wife of the Roman Emperor, Macsen Wledig (Magnus Maximus). According to the story, one day whilst out hunting he dreamt of a beautiful lady in a far off land. When he awoke, he was haunted by his dream and his counsels advised him to send messengers to look for her. They wandered the world until eventually they found her at Aber Saint (near Caernarfon). The emperor came to Wales to marry Elen, and carried out her request for a road linking North and South Wales – hence Sarn Helen.

4. The small steep mound of the Bryn y Castell Iron Age hillfort is to the left of the track. Pass the highest part of the hill before climbing to the flat top, which is surrounded by a stone rampart. A stone round hut lies in the north corner, and cobbles and post holes in the middle of the site indicate the position of wooden round houses. Excavation over several years revealed much evidence of iron working. It is thought the hill-fort was occupied from about 300BC until the arrival of the Romans. The hill commands extensive views of the surrounding moorland.

5. According to legend, the men of Ardudwy were buried here, after a battle near Llyn Morwynion on the Migneint moor. There was a shortage of women in Ardudwy, and the men raided Dyffryn Clwyd capturing several young maidens. Armed men of Clwyd followed them, and all the Ardudwy men were killed and later buried here, near Sarn Helen. According to the legend, the maidens had fallen in love with their captors and rather than return to Clwyd, they drowned themselves in Llyn Morwynion (Lake of the Maidens). There are records of graves here. Robert Vaughan of Hengwrt (1592-1667)

reports their existence, and according to a 17th century edition of *Britannia* there were at least 30 of them, each about two yards long with a short pillar at each corner. Pennant in his *Tour of Wales*, found that most of the stones were removed. By 1851, just two headstones remained and 60 years later, only mounds were noticeable. The stones have probably been used for making nearby walls.

6. The Cynfal Waterfall (Rhaeadr Cynfal) is not very high, but it falls in a spectacular arch. Steps and a handrail permit safe viewing. Nearby, in the middle of the river, stands a column of rock known as Pulpud Huw Llwyd. At the time of James I, Huw Llwyd, an ex-soldier and sorcerer, lived at the nearby house Cynfal Fawr. He used the rock for poetry, preaching sermons and devil-raising spells. Huw claimed that he was safe from evil when he was on the rock, because the devil was afraid of water. Thomas Love Peacock gives an account of this devil-raising in his novel *Headlong Hall*. Before he died in 1630, Huw asked his daughter to throw all his books on magic into the gorge. As they reached the surface, a hand rose from the depths and drew the books into the darkness of the water.

Walk Directions: (-) denotes Point of Interest

1. In the square at Llan Ffestiniog (1), have the Pengwern Arms on your right and the church on your left, then take a lane downhill in the direction of the Moelwyn mountains. The lane bends to the right, and in another 40 metres ignore a kissing-gate on the left. Go through the gate next to it, and descend the field near a fence on the left.

2. Cross a stile and turn left through a small gate. Continue downhill bearing right to a broad gate. Continue to descend beside a fence on the left. Go through two gates near a house and follow the track downhill to a gate in the left corner of the field.

3. Turn right on a track between walls. When it meets another track turn right and, in a few paces, bear left past a ruined barn. Descend the field and cross a footbridge over Afon Teigl.

4. The path bears left and away from the river. When it reaches another footbridge, ignore it and turn right to go uphill through conifers.

5. The river is now below on your right. The path descends to cross a stream, rises again, then descends a little before swinging to the right, uphill, and crossing a stile.

6. Keep ahead on a path, and go through a wall gap on to a track. This used to be the main road from Tanygrisiau to Llan Ffestiniog. The bridge over the river was destroyed about 100 years ago. Bear right for a few paces and cross a stile. Continue beside the river, passing a number of small waterfalls. At a house, follow a fence on your left and reach a lane.

7. Turn right, ignoring a lane on the left and a track on the right. Cross the A470 and turn left. In 40 metres, cross a ladder stile and bear slightly right across the field. Go up steps to the left of a tall telegraph pole. Cross the railway line and keep ahead, past another pole, to gates and a lane.

8. Turn left and follow the lane past cottages and a chapel. The mountain on your left is Manod Mawr. At a fork, go through the right-hand gate and follow this lane through Cwm Teigl for nearly 800 metres to reach a two-way footpath signpost. As this right of way is presently blocked, continue on the lane, shortly turn right on a track and go through a gate.

9. The right of way joins the track. Pass a house, Hafod Ysbyty (2), on your left, go through a gate and cross a footbridge over the Afon Gamallt. Bear left over a wall, and head uphill with the wall on your right. Pass an old building on the right, and go through the gate ahead to follow a green track.

10. Near the top of the rise, another track joins from the left. This is Sarn Helen (3), the Roman Road. Keep ahead for 40 metres to a track junction. To visit Bryn y Castell (4), turn left for 500 metres.

11. Retrace your steps on the track, and continue downhill past the Water Board buildings. The Graves of the Men of Ardudwy (5) are on the slope below the waterworks. At the B4391, turn right and almost immediately left on a lane. Follow it to the A470 at Bontnewydd.

12. Turn left and then right to have the river, Afon Cynfal, on your right. When the lane divides, take the right fork. In 70 metres (before a

wall is met on the right) turn right over a stile, and follow the path through coniferous trees.

13. Cross a wall and keep ahead on the main path through woodland and above the river. Go under a bridge, beside a wall and descend to a viewpoint of a waterfall.

14. Continue beside the river and join other paths at a fence and wall. Turn right to cross a footbridge over Afon Cynfal. Follow the path through trees to ladder stiles. Turn left on a path with white arrows to view the waterfall, Rhaeadr Cynfal (6).

15. Return to the path, turn left over a stile and follow a wall on the right. Continue beside a fence to a gate near barns. Turn right and, in a few paces, turn left through a small gate.

16. Follow the wall to another gate, descend to cross a plank bridge, go through a gate, and cross the field to a kissing-gate on the right-hand side of a building. Go uphill beside the fence to the road. Turn right to the starting point in Llan Ffestiniog.

Facilities:

Public toilets in the village. Refreshments at the Pengwern Arms near the start and Myfanwy's in Blaenau Ffestiniog. Llechwedd Slate Caverns. Ffestiniog Railway.

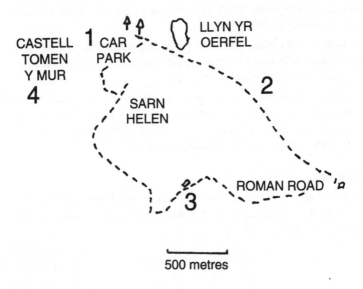

CASTELL
TOMEN
Y MUR
4

1 CAR
PARK

LLYN YR
OERFEL

SARN
HELEN

2

ROMAN ROAD

3

500 metres

Castell Tomen y Mur – Llyn yr Oerfel – Dolbelydr – Roman Road – Castell Tomen y Mur

OS Maps:	1:50 000 Landranger Sheet 124; 1:25 000 Outdoor Leisure Sheet 18.
Start:	Lane end near Roman amphitheatre. G.R. 708389.
Access:	Leave the A470 north of Trawsfynydd on a lane east. This is shortly before the road's junction with the A487. Follow the lane under a railway bridge for 1.5km to a parking area. Buses from Blaenau Ffestiniog and Dolgellau to Gellilydan, 2.5km from the start.
Parking:	Lane end near the Roman amphitheatre.
Grade:	Easy – mainly tracks.
Time:	2-2½ hours.

Points of Interest:

1. Built in the first century AD, the small Roman amphitheatre, with its high circular banks, is not difficult to find. It is thought to be the only amphitheatre attached to an auxiliary fort in Britain. However, there are doubts whether it was used as a true amphitheatre, a theatre. It may have been used purely for weapons training.

2. Barracks, mill ruins and a tramway with a bridge are the most interesting visible remains of Braich-ddu slate quarry. The mill was powered by a waterwheel, and the finished slate was carried along the tramway and then carried in carts to the quays on Afon Dwyryd near Maentwrog.

3. Trawsfynydd is a man-made lake. Formerly in the valley there was a large bog, Cors Goch, several small farms and a chapel. Between 1924-1928 a dam was built, to provide piped water to the Maentwrog

hydro-electric power station in the Vale of Ffestiniog. In the 1960s the lake was enlarged when the nuclear power station was built. Warm water from the station took eight days to flow around the lake, which is nearly three miles long. The nuclear power station is now being de-commissioned. A latex castle was erected on one of the lake's islands for the filming of 'First Knight' starring Sean Connery and Richard Gere.

4. The large mound that you can see is actually a Norman motte built across the wall of the Roman fort. The original fort of AD78 was constructed of timber and turf, and occupied 1.7ha. Forty years later a slightly smaller fort was built in stone, but it was abandoned about AD140. The approach is by the south-east gate, where excavations have revealed the guard chambers. Walk to the left (SW) to see the earth banks of the original fort. Built across the western rampart of the reduced fort and surrounded by a ditch, the 11th century motte may have been built by William Rufus. In Y Mabinogion, Lleu had a court here but his unfaithful wife Blodeuwedd wanted him dead. By guile she discovered how he might be slain, and her lover Gronw killed him with a poisoned dart on the bank of Afon Cynfal. Lleu was restored to life by the magician Gwydion, and he met his rival again on the river bank. Although Gronw had a stone to protect himself, Lleu's dart pierced not only the slab but also Gronw. The stone exists on a hill above the valley. Meanwhile, Gwydion turned the escaping Blodeuwedd into an owl, and her maidens drowned in Llyn Morwynion (Lake of the Maidens).

Walk Directions: (-) denotes Point of Interest

1. From the parking place, continue along the lane on to a track. Pass the Roman amphitheatre (1) on the right and in a few metres, take a track with a walking man signpost. (Ignore another track to the right of it, unless you want to visit Castell Tomen y Mur first.) Follow the track uphill through moorland, and in 250 metres ignore a track on the left.

2. Keep ahead past Llyn yr Oerfel. A dismantled tramway is visible to the right of the track, and in less than 800 metres you reach the

remains of Braich-ddu quarry (2).

3. Continue on the track, which becomes a grassy path. It descends to a ruin (Dolbelydr) at some sheepfolds, near a small waterfall. Here another track joins from the right.

4. Turn right and follow this track, which is the Roman Road between Segontium (the Roman fort at Caernarfon) and Caer Gai near Llyn Tegid (Bala Lake). Continue through a gate and pass under the wires between pylons. Bear to the right with the track, and in another 600 metres turn left through a gate.

5. Keep ahead on the track, and go through gates at Llwyn-crwn farm. Pass the farmhouse on the right, and continue downhill with fine views towards Trawsfynydd Lake (3).

6. The track bears right and in another 120 metres, shortly before it reaches a bridge, turn right on a track, presently enclosed by walls. Although Ordnance Survey maps show a different line, this old trackway is probably Sarn Helen, the Roman Road which started at Canovium, Caerhun (in the Conwy valley) and finished at Maridunum, Caerfyrddin.

7. When the wall ends, keep ahead to cross a stream, and continue on a walled track. Pass an old barn on the left, keep ahead through gates, and pass close to a pylon. Pass another ruin on the right and after the next gate, turn left to cross a stream.

8. Follow the track uphill with a wall on the left. Look for a small gate in the wall. This gives access to Castell Tomen y Mur. However, first continue through the gate ahead for about 80 metres, to view the wide level area of the Roman parade ground.

9. Return and go through the small gate. A few metres downstream is an embankment which supported the bridge on the Roman road. Pass the remains of the bathhouse, and walk towards the mound (4).

10. Leave by the north-east gate near a ruined farmhouse. Follow a wide path to a gate and track. Keep ahead on this, and bear left to the amphitheatre and starting point.

Facilities:

Pubs in Trawsfynydd, Gellilydan, Llan Ffestiniog and Maentwrog.

Tyddyn Gwladys – Pistyll Cain
– Rhaeadr Mawddach – Tyddyn Gwladys

OS Maps:	1:50 000 Landranger Sheet 124; 1:25 000 Outdoor Leisure Sheet 18.
Start:	Tyddyn Gwladys car park, G.R. 735263.
Access:	Take the A470 to the village of Ganllwyd, 5 miles north of Dolgellau. At the northern end of the village take a lane east (to the right if travelling from Dolgellau), for 2km to the car park. Buses from Dolgellau and Blaenau Ffestiniog to Ganllwyd, 2.5km from the start.
Parking:	Tyddyn Gwladys car park in Coed-y-Brenin.
Grade:	Easy – forest tracks and paths.
Time:	2-2½ hours.

Points of Interest:

1. Coed-y-Brenin was formerly part of the Nannau Estate which was founded about AD1100 by Cadwgan, son of the Prince of Powys. The land remained in the same family for more than 600 years. In the 18th century it passed to the Vaughan family through marriage. After the First World War, land was purchased from the estate for forestry, and it was named the Vaughan Forest. In 1935, to commemorate the Silver Jubilee of King George V and Queen Mary, the name was changed to Coed-y-Brenin – Forest of the King. The area covered by Coed-y-Brenin is around 3500 acres, and nearly three quarters of this is woodland. About 40,000 tonnes of timber are harvested each year from 28-35 acres of felled conifers. Red squirrels are here and, in summer, pied flycatchers. A herd of fallow deer from the former estate may be seen on open ground in Coed-y-Brenin. Long ago these deer helped a holy man who lived in the forest. According to the legend, his ox was killed by a fallen tree and he could no longer plough to grow

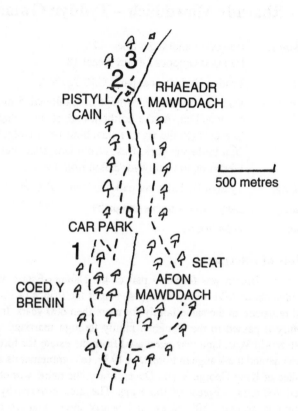

PISTYLL
CAIN

RHAEADR
MAWDDACH

CAR PARK

COED Y
BRENIN

AFON
MAWDDACH

SEAT

500 metres

his food. The wild deer saw this and attached themselves to the plough and turned the soil. Wolves followed behind dragging the harrows, and the holy man was able to sow.

2. The Gwynfynydd mine was originally worked for lead, until gold was discovered in 1864 and it became the second most important mine in the Meirionnydd goldfield. Pritchard Morgan, the Gold King, developed the mine after gaining gold prospecting experience in Australia. Within a few years of floating the 'Morgan Gold Mine Company' £14,000 worth of gold had been extracted. More than 200 men were employed, many of them having to walk long distances to work. Some lodged on farms, others in barracks. The ore was crushed to powder by stamp mills, sieved and amalgamated with mercury, then separated. Another method involved washing the ore over sloping tables covered with coarse corduroy, the gold caught in the grooves whilst the rock dust was washed away. Prosperity was short lived. The Gwynfynydd and Clogau mines were amalgamated in 1900 but the Gwynfynydd mine had to close in 1916. There has been a revival, and mining operations again take place. Occasionally it is open to visitors. The gold is used for jewellery, including rings for the Royal family.

3. Rhaeadr Mawddach is a little higher up the river from where Afon Cain joins the Mawddach. Under the Mawddach waterfall, a waterwheel provided power for the Gwynfynydd gold mine. The source of the Mawddach is on high moors west of Llyn Tegid (Bala Lake).

Walk Directions: (-) denotes Point of Interest

1. From the Tyddyn Gwladys car park in Coed-y-Brenin (1) continue along the lane and when it ends, keep ahead on a track, signed Private Track and No Through Road.

2. The track passes above Afon Mawddach. Go round a barrier, and walk behind the houses known as Ferndale. Continue on the track, and shortly after it bends left there is a view of a waterfall, Rhaeadr Mawddach.

3. The track bends right across a bridge over Afon Cain. From the far

side of the bridge, take a rough path up the ravine for a closer view of another waterfall, Pistyll Cain.

4. Return to the bridge and turn left. In a few metres you will reach the site of the Gwynfynydd Gold Mine Mill (2).

5. Continue on the track passing above Rhaeadr Mawddach (3). Shortly beyond the waterfall, the walk crosses a bridge on the right. If you wish to see Gwynfynydd mine, before crossing the bridge follow the track about 350 metres to the mine. Do not enter! Return the same way.

6. After crossing the bridge, follow the track uphill to a junction. Turn right and you will shortly reach an open space with views of both waterfalls. A little further on, Ferndale is in view on the opposite bank of the river.

7. At a fork in the track turn left, uphill. A track joins from the left. Continue to a post with the number 12. On the left there is a seat. Here turn right, downhill, on a track. It crosses a stream and continues to descend with the stream on your right.

8. Reach another track and turn left, with Afon Mawddach below on the right. In a few paces, turn right over a footbridge and walk up to the lane.

9. Turn right and in 50 metres turn left on a narrow path opposite a yellow topped post. The path rises gradually through the forest and reaches a track at post 36.

10. Turn right on the track and follow it downhill to rejoin the lane. Turn left to the car park and picnic area at the starting point.

Facilities:

Picnic tables at the car park. Public toilets in Ganllwyd. Coed-y-Brenin Visitor Centre and Cafe (Easter-October), 2 miles north of Ganllwyd. Forest map available for exploring other paths and tracks in Coed-y-Brenin. Mountain bike trails. All facilities in Dolgellau.

Ganllwyd – Rhaeadr Ddu – Coed Ganllwyd – Cefn-coch Gold Mine – Dolmelynllyn – Ganllwyd

OS Maps:	1:50 000 Landranger Sheet 124; 1:25 000 Outdoor Leisure Sheet 18.
Start:	Ganllwyd car park, G.R. 726243.
Access:	Ganllwyd is on the A470, north of Dolgellau. The car park is on the southern side of the village. Buses from Dolgellau and Blaenau Ffestiniog.
Parking:	Car park in Ganllwyd.
Grade:	Easy/Moderate – woodland and hillside paths, tracks and lane.
Time:	2-2½ hours.

Points of Interest:

1. The poem is by Thomas Gray and the original inscription was carved into a nearby rock. Thomas Gray is better known for his 'Elegy Written in a Country Churchyard'. William Alexander Madocks (1773-1828), who lived at Dolmelynllyn, may have been responsible for the carving. Many poets stayed at Dolmelynllyn and visited the waterfalls, which are on the estate. Madocks, keenly interested in landscape design and town planning, created Porthmadog, Tremadog and The Cob embankment.

2. Rhaeadr Ddu is sited inside Coed Ganllwyd, a nature reserve. The spray from the falls and the high rainfall provide ideal conditions for mosses, liverworts and ferns. This is an ancient oak woodland, and the dominant tree is the sessile oak with some ash and birch. Alder buckthorn grows on the reserve, providing food for the caterpillars of the uncommon yellow butterfly, the brimstone. Look and listen for pied flycatchers, jays and other woodland birds.

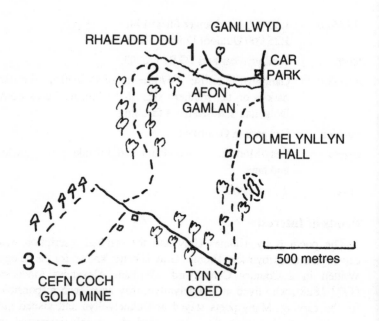

GANLLWYD

RHAEADR DDU

1

CAR PARK

2

AFON GAMLAN

DOLMELYNLLYN HALL

500 metres

3

CEFN COCH GOLD MINE

TYN Y COED

3. The third richest of the Meirionnydd gold mines, Cefn-coch operated between 1862 and 1914. Gold was discovered in the Mawddach valley during the 1840s, when the Cwm-heisan mines (near Gwynfynydd in Coed-y-Brenin) were being worked for lead. A yellow metal caught in the dressing machine was identified as gold. The gold belt stretched from near Barmouth, east along the Mawddach estuary to Bontddu, and then north almost to Trawsfynydd. At first, ore at Cefn-coch was processed at the stamping mill near the stream. Later it was taken downhill by tramway to Berthlwyd, where the plant had a steam engine. Unfortunately, the workings became unproductive and the company wound up in 1866. The mine was worked again briefly, ten years later. The next revival was in the 1890's when a new company built a large mill. The ore was carried from the main adit by a level tramway. Almost 1,400oz of gold had been extracted when the mine finally closed in 1914.

Walk Directions: (-) denotes Point of Interest

1. From Ganllwyd car park, walk across to the information board and follow a path to the A470. Turn left and, before crossing the bridge over Afon Gamlan, turn right onto a gated lane.

2. In about 200 metres where the lane turns right, leave the lane, and keep ahead to a marker post in the trees. Follow the main path to the next marker post then keep ahead on a narrow path to a view of the falls, Rhaeadr Ddu, at a stone inscribed with a poem (1).

3. Return to the post, and descend to cross the footbridge over the river. Keep ahead to a path, and turn right to follow a rough path which climbs above two waterfalls (2).

4. Look for a marker post and a path that enters the woods. The path reaches, and follows, a wall on your right. Ignore a ladder stile and continue on the path, now further away from the wall. Go through a kissing-gate and at a path junction, turn right.

5. In about 25 metres, turn left through a gate and cross a footbridge. Bear right, uphill, to a lane. Turn right, go through a gate and continue about 80 metres to take a track on the left. In a few paces, at a fork, go left again.

6. When a forest road is met on the right, ignore it. Keep to the left, on the track nearest the wall. Shortly, cross a stile and plank bridge on the left. Follow the path to a marker post on a wide track.

7. Turn left to pass the ruins of Cefn-coch gold mine (3). On the right is the crushing mill and on the left are the barracks. Continue to a high ladder stile on the left. Cross the stile and descend the field, following marker posts. Cross another stile in a wall, and keep ahead to a small ruin. Pass it on your right and cross a stile near a gate. Continue to a lane.

8. Turn right to pass Berthlwyd, and follow the lane downhill for about 500 metres to a house called Tyn-y-coed. Immediately after passing the house, turn left through a small gate and follow the left fence to a gate that leads into woodland.

9. Follow the path through another gate, and reach a track. Here, a diversion can be made to visit an ornamental lake. Turn right about 120 metres to a waymarked post. Bear left to take the path around the lake, and cross a footbridge before returning to the track.

10. After visiting the lake, turn right on the track and follow it past Dolmelynllyn Hall to a junction. Keep ahead and continue on the drive to the A470. Turn left to the starting point.

Facilities:

Guide available for exploring the Dolmelynllyn Estate, which is owned by the National Trust. Toilets in the car park at the start. Full facilities in Dolgellau.

Nannau – Precipice Walk
– Llyn Cynwch – Nannau

OS Maps:	1:50 000 Landranger Sheet 124; 1:25 000 Outdoor Leisure Sheet 18.
Start:	Car park 1 mile south of Llanfachreth. G.R. 745211.
Access:	From Dolgellau cross the bridge over the Afon Wnion and turn right. In 700 metres turn left on the road for Llanfachreth. In 2 miles you will pass Nannau Farm. The car park is another 300 metres on the left. Buses – infrequent – to Llanfachreth pass the car park.
Parking:	Snowdonia National Park car park at the start of the walk.
Grade:	Easy – fairly level hill and lakeside paths and tracks.
Time:	2 hours.

Points of Interest:

1. Cadwgan, a descendant of the Prince of Powys, built the first Nannau house in the early 12th century. He was killed at Welshpool, but the land was passed through the male line for 500 years. An effigy of one of the descendants, Meurig ap Ynyr Fychan, is in Dolgellau church. The family co-operated with the English conquerors and this led to trouble with Owain Glyndŵr, who burned down the Nannau house. According to one story, Hywel Sele (8th Lord of Nannau) and Owain Glyndŵr were out hunting together in order to settle their differences, and Hywel shot an arrow at Owain. The arrow bounced off Owain because he wrote a breast plate. In the fight that followed, Owain killed Hywel and hid his body in a tree before burning down the house. The body remained there for many years before it was found. In the early 17th century, Huw Nanney was jailed in Fleet Prison for felling 10,000 oaks and not paying a fine of £1000.

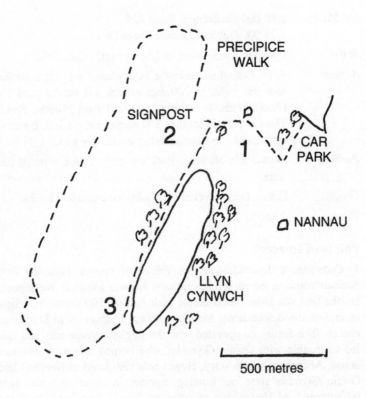

PRECIPICE
WALK

SIGNPOST

2

1

CAR
PARK

NANNAU

LLYN
CYNWCH

3

500 metres

Eventually he paid £800, and after his release he rebuilt Nannau. The present house was built by Colonel Huw Nanney in 1693 and when he died, because he left no sons, the line came to an end. His daughters married into the Vaughan family. The immense drystone walls on the estate are the work of Robert Vaughan (1768-1843) who kept a large team of horses, mules and carters for the work. The Vaughans still run the estate, although they have not lived in the house since 1966.

2. On the Nannau estate, the Precipice Walk opened to the public in 1890, and it has become a popular and well-known walk. It probably originated as a path made by sheep, and became wider with human use. A fairly level path, it keeps roughly to the 800 foot contour. The precipitous part of the walk runs above the Mawddach valley, and on clear days gives outstanding views.

3. Llyn Cynwch is a popular lake with fishermen. According to legend, many years ago the local people were terrified of a massive serpent that lived near the lake. People and animals who looked at the monster's eyes were paralysed and eaten. The lord of Nannau offered sixty cattle as a reward to the person who could destroy it. After a long period of time, a shepherd found the serpent sleeping and killed it. The creature is said to be buried on the mountainside.

Walk Directions: (-) denotes Point of Interest

1. Starting from the car park, turn left on the lane in the direction of Hermon. In 100 metres, turn left on a track into a wood.

2. In 200 metres, follow the track as it bends right. Continue with a fence and field on the left. At a corner of the fence, turn left to pass a cottage on the right. If you look to the left you will see Nannau House (1).

3. Cross a stile, and follow the path to the right through trees. Cross another stile in the left fence and keep ahead, following a wall on the right to a signpost for the Precipice Walk (2).

4. Turn right, following the path beside the wall. It eventually curves to the left and contours the hillside high above the Mawddach valley. Look for information boards describing the vegetation, land use and scenery.

5. At the southern end of the path there are fine views of the Mawddach estuary, Cadair Idris and Dolgellau. The path swings left, north-east, to reach a lake, Llyn Cynwch (3).

6. Keep the lake on your right, and just beyond it you will rejoin your outward route. Retrace your steps to the start at the car park.

Facilities:

Toilets in the car park. Full facilities in Dolgellau.

Afon Clywedog – Torrent Walk – Brithdir – Afon Clywedog

OS Maps:	1:50 000 Landranger Sheet 124; 1:25 000 Outdoor Leisure Sheet 23.
Start:	Small lay-by on the B4416 to the south-west of Brithdir, G.R. 761181.
Access:	3km east of Dolgellau, leave the A470 to take the B4416. Cross a bridge over Afon Clywedog, and continue to a layby on the left. The A470 is on the Machynlleth-Dolgellau bus route.
Parking:	Small lay-by near the start of the Torrent Walk.
Grade:	Easy – woodland path above river, lanes and tracks.
Time:	About 2 hours.

Points of Interest:

1. Thomas Payne designed the Torrent Walk, and also the long embankment across the estuary at Porthmadog. There were two paths, one on each side of the Afon Clywedog ravine, but the other has been lost through erosion and extreme plant growth. The walk was commissioned by Baron Richards (1752-1823) of Caerynwch, as an extension to the mansion's gardens.

2. The Afon Clywedog rushes and tumbles through broad-leaved woodland of oak, beech, ash and lime. In about 300 metres, and close to beech trees, look for a bench overlooking the river. Provided by the North Wales Wildlife Trust, it is a memorial to the local botanist Mrs Mary Richards (1885-1977) of Caerynwch. With Peter Benoit she wrote 'Contribution to a Flora of Merioneth' (1963) but she also travelled extensively abroad, especially in Africa, where she collected specimens for Kew. In recognition of her botanical work, she was awarded with an MBE in 1969.

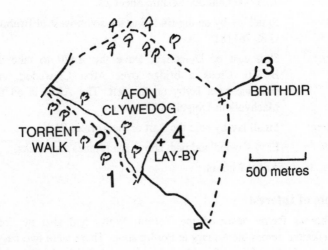

TORRENT
WALK

AFON
CLYWEDOG

BRITHDIR

LAY-BY

500 metres

3. A Roman road goes through Brithdir, which has a small Roman fort. To view the fort (which has no public access, but is visible from the road), continue to the village. Ignore the left descending road, but keep ahead on a lane. The site is on the left, a flat square with ramparts on the eastern side.

4. St Mark's Church, Brithdir, was built in 1885 after the death of the Rev. Charles Tooth, who was founder and chaplain of St Mark's Church in Florence. He wanted all his possessions to be sold after his death and the proceeds used for the Christian Church. His widow, Louisa Tooth, had already inherited property in Brithdir, and she carried out her husband's wishes by the building of this church. Although built of local stone, the style of the church is Italian. One of the architects was Henry Wilson of the art nouveau movement. The domed blue ceiling contrasts effectively with the red ochre of the sanctuary and chancel walls. The doors are of teak, and the lead font has a medieval design. Most remarkable is the beaten copper which has been used in the making of the pulpit and altar, thought to be the only ones so treated in Wales. The Spanish chestnut choir stalls are decorated with carvings of animals. Mrs Richards was responsible for the planting of the rhododendrons in the churchyard.

Walk Directions: (-) denotes Point of Interest

1. From the lay-by, return along the B4416 in the direction of the A470. Pass a lane on the left, and continue to a footpath signpost on the right. Go through a kissing-gate, signposted Torrent Walk (1).

2. Follow the wide woodland path above the tumbling river, Afon Clywedog (2).

3. Emerge on a lane and turn right. Ignore a lane on the right, going uphill. (The usual return to the start of the Torrent Walk.)

4. When the lane bends left, keep ahead through a gate and follow a track. Go through another gate, and continue through the forest to a fork. Ignore the left descending track, which crosses a cattle grid. Keep ahead a few paces, then bear right uphill, through the forest.

5. At a fork, keep a wall on the left. The track becomes grassy. Go

ahead through a gate and follow the track to another gate. Keep ahead on the access lane to the B4416, and turn left in the direction of Brithdir village (3).

6. Pass a chapel and immediately turn right. Follow this lane past Cefn-y-maes, and go through a gate. Pass another house, and continue on a grassy track to a gate. Cross to another gate, and walk along the clear track uphill.

7. Go through a gate on to a walled track, and follow it to a lane.

8. Turn right on the lane, downhill, to the B4416. Turn right to the lay-by at the starting point. Continue along the road for 300 metres if you wish to see St Mark's Church (4).

Facilities:

Cross Foxes Inn 1.5km south on the A470. Full facilities in Dolgellau.

Dolgellau – Afon Aran – Quaker Cemetery – Tabor – Esgeiriau – Dolgellau

OS Maps:	1:50 000 Landranger Sheet 124; 1:25 000 Outdoor Leisure Sheet 23.
Start:	Car park near the bridge over Afon Wnion in Dolgellau, G.R. 728179.
Access:	Dolgellau is on the A470, north of Machynlleth. Buses from Wrexham, Barmouth, Tywyn, Machynlleth, Aberystwyth and Blaenau Ffestiniog.
Parking:	Large car park near Afon Wnion.
Grade:	Moderate – tracks and lanes.
Time:	3-3½ hours.

Points of Interest:

1. Magnificently sited beneath Cadair Idris and on Afon Wnion, the small town of Dolgellau is a maze of narrow lanes and historic buildings. The bridge over the river was built in 1638, the old town hall (now a restaurant) dates back to 1606 and the buildings in Eldon Square are around 200 years old. St Mary's Church has wooden pillars brought by oxcart from the forests of Dinas Mawddwy and an effigy of Meurig ap Ynyr Fychan of Nannau who died in 1350. The ironmongers (T.H. Roberts) is on the site of Cwrt Plas yn Dre, which was a meeting place for Owain Glyndŵr. Dolgellau was a centre for the woollen industry, and in the 18th century at least sixty fulling mills (pandai) operated alongside the fast flowing streams of Meirionnydd. It was a domestic occupation, with almost every cottager and small farmer near Dolgellau owning a hand loom. The cloth produced, known as 'Welsh plains and cottons', was used for clothing armies, and it was also sent to North America. The bales of cloth, webs, were exported from Barmouth. When weaving became a factory industry in

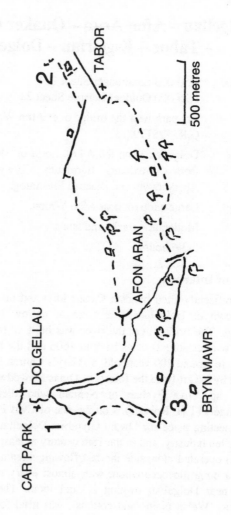

CAR PARK

DOLGELLAU

TABOR

AFON ARAN

BRYN MAWR

1

2

3

500 metres

the early 19th century some carding mills were built in Meirionnydd, but loss of markets forced the mills to close.

2. Owen Lewis of Tyddyngarreg provided the Quakers with this burial ground. He was one of the first to be converted when the Quaker George Fox came to Dolgellau in 1657. Tyddyngarreg was a regular meeting place for the Quakers, as also was Dolserau. The message of George Fox was that man did not need rites and church hierarchies to reach God. Because they would not take any kind of oath, the Quakers were persecuted and several spent time in prison, including Robert Owen of Dolserau. When William Penn acquired land in America in 1681, the Welsh Quakers bought 40,000 acres there. Hundreds of Welsh Quakers emigrated to Pennsylvania. Quakers were discouraged from using stones on their graves, and the rather elaborate stones now in the burial ground at Tyddyngarreg belong to the Independents.

3. Rowland Ellis of Bryn-mawr became a Quaker in 1672 and before long he was arrested and taken to prison at Bala. When he and others refused to take the Oath of Allegiance, Judge Walcott treated them as traitors. For punishment the men were to be hung, drawn and quartered and the women burnt but, luckily, a London lawyer proved that the law no longer applied and the prisoners were set free. Rowland Ellis sailed to Pennsylvania in 1686. He named his new farm Bryn-mawr, and this name was later given to a women's college there, although it is not on the same site.

Walk Directions: (-) denotes Point of Interest

1. From the car park near Afon Wnion in Dolgellau (1), take the footpath that passes Yr Efail Restaurant. Bear right then left, and keep ahead to Eldon Square.

2. Walk through the square, then turn left. Pass Clifton House Hotel on the right, and follow the road as it bears to the right. Cross a bridge over Afon Aran.

3. Immediately turn right, with the river nearby on your right and houses on your left. Join a road and keep ahead to its end. Take the right-hand track, uphill.

4. The track becomes grassy with open views of a valley below, on your right. Continue on this track until it joins a lane. Turn left and in 60 metres, at a left bend, turn right on a track (signposted bridleway).

5. Follow a stream, and cross a cattle grid into a field. After passing some houses, cross a stream and go through a broad gate. Turn left to follow a wall on the left.

6. Reach a marker post, go through a wall gap, and cross the stream again. Bear right uphill on a path through woodland. Go through a gate, and continue near a wall on the right. At the end of the field, just left of the field corner, cross a stile. There are good views from here of Cadair Idris.

7. Turn left and follow a track past a building, and shortly a house on the left. The track bears right, and after crossing a cattle grid, it turns left into a lane.

8. Turn right, and pass Fronolau Restaurant. Continue another 200 metres and at a footpath signpost, turn left on a track through a gate.

9. Follow this enclosed track, and at a house, bear right to stay on the track as it passes between trees and rhododendrons. Go through a gate and pass a house. In another 150 metres, reach a footpath signpost.

10. Turn left past farm buildings and pass a house. In a few metres, at another signpost, go left through a gate and follow the wall. In 80 metres, it reaches a small gate leading into the Quaker Burial Ground (2).

11. Return through the field, turn right to pass the house, and reach the track left earlier. Turn left along the track to a lane. Bear right to a lane junction.

12. Turn left on this lane. On your left is Tabor Chapel (formerly a Quaker Meeting House). In 80 metres, turn right on a track leading to a stile at a gate.

13. Follow the track, which bears left and passes walled fields on the right. In about 650 metres, take a path on the right. (This is about 120 metres before the track reaches the forest.) Follow a wall for 15 metres then, where the wall bends right, continue on a clear path.

14. When the path divides, take the left fork and follow it to a gate. Continue on a walled track, and when a track joins from the left, bear right. Pass a house, continue on a track, and descend to a gate.

15. Follow the track through open fields and trees. Ignore a right-hand track, and keep ahead to a lane.

16. Turn left on the lane, with Afon Aran on your right. In a few metres, at a fork, bear right and cross a bridge over the river. Follow the wooded lane past Parc Cottage and the drive to Bryn-mawr (3).

17. In another 350 metres, at a dip in the lane where it crosses a stream (Nant y Ceunant), go through a gate on the right to follow a bridleway. The path bears left, uphill, and then descends. Before reaching a wall, bear right and continue to a gate on the left.

18. Follow the enclosed track which makes a steep descent, and ignore footpaths leading off it. At houses, bear right on a track downhill to meet a lane. Turn right, and at a road junction, keep ahead to pass the Catholic Church. Turn left to the square, and retrace your steps to the starting point.

Facilities:

Public toilets near the start of the walk. Fronolau Restaurant on the walk. Full facilities in Dolgellau. Exhibitions at the Tourist Information Centre in Dolgellau.

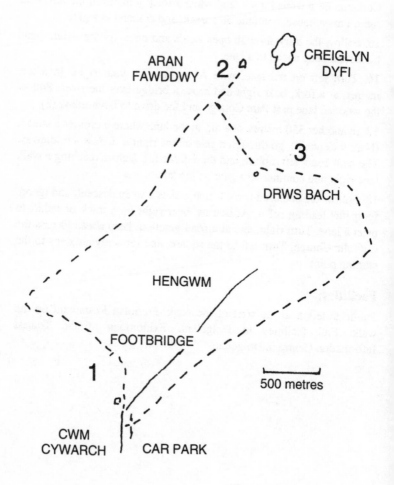

CREIGLYN DYFI

ARAN FAWDDWY

2

3

DRWS BACH

HENGWM

FOOTBRIDGE

1

500 metres

CWM CYWARCH

CAR PARK

Walk 20   *7½ miles/11.5 kilometres*

Cwm Cywarch – Aran Fawddwy – Drws-bach – Hengwm – Cwm Cywarch

OS Maps:	1:50 000 Landranger Sheet 124; 1:25 000 Outdoor Leisure Sheet 23.
Start:	Cwm Cywarch, G.R. 853184.
Access:	Leave the A470 at Dinas Mawddwy and take the minor road for Llanymawddwy. Turn left at houses in 1.5km. Parking area 4km. Infrequent buses from Dolgellau to Dinas Mawddwy.
Parking:	At end of common in Cwm Cywarch.
Grade:	Strenuous – mountain paths, some rocky. The ascent uses a courtesy path – dogs not allowed.
Time:	5½-6 hours.

Points of Interest:

1. Lead mining may have taken place during Roman times at a site near the Brynhafod climbers' hut. Near the path, the Cywarch mine was worked in the late 18th century, producing only about 80 tons. Another attempt was made about eighty years later with more investment, but over a period of nearly twenty years the mine produced less than 350 tons.

2. Aran Fawddwy at 905 metres (2,971 feet) is the highest peak in Meirionnydd. The summit is marked by a great pile of stones, said to have been placed there by the men of Dinas Mawddwy when they were told that Cadair Idris was higher. Cadair Idris, however, is lower by fourteen metres (44 feet). On the 10th of February, 1945, a Bristol Beaufighter flew into this mountain in low cloud, killing its crew. On a clear day the views from the summit are superb – Cadair Idris, Rhinogydd, Snowdon, Arenig Fawr, Berwyn and Pumlumon. The ridge runs north for 2.5km to Aran Benllyn (885m), before dropping to

Llanuwchllyn near Llyn Tegid (Bala Lake). The high cliffs of Aran Fawddwy shelter Creiglyn Dyfi, the source of Afon Dyfi, a lovely river which meanders thirty miles before reaching the sea at Aberdyfi. The stream which drains the lake is called the Llaethnant (milk stream), because of its foamy water. According to one legend, Saint Decho who lived in the valley turned the stream into milk.

3. Drws-bach means little door, the door to Aran Fawddwy. The cairn is in memory of Michael Robert Aspain, a member of RAF St Athan mountain rescue. He was killed by lightning near here in June, 1960, whilst on duty. His team built the cairn. You may wish to sign the book in the heavy box. In 1944, a De Haviland Mosquito of 540 squadron crashed close by, killing the crew of two.

Walk Directions: (-) denotes Point of Interest

1. Starting from the parking area in Cwm Cywarch, continue along the lane. Ignore the footbridge over the river, but just before Blaencywarch Farm, turn right through a kissing-gate.

2. Continue to a track, and then bear left. In a few paces turn right through a gate, and follow a wall on the left. Continue over stiles, and at the end of the wall, turn left to cross another stile. Keep ahead for about 25 metres, and then bear right on a path.

3. The path climbs through the valley past the site of an old lead mine (1). After crossing a footbridge over a stream the path becomes steeper and, in places, slippery. Look for yellow arrows on the rocks.

4. Eventually the path eases and reaches a fence. Keep it on your left, and pass a ruin. In another 600 metres, bear right to leave the fence at a signpost for Aran Fawddwy. Pass in front of a peaty pool, and follow white topped posts to a stile.

5. Cross the stile and follow the fence on the right. Cross two stiles close together, and continue with the fence now on the left. Go over another stile, keeping the fence on your left, and continue beside the fence (ignoring stiles in the fence), until a stile is crossed in a corner, just below the south top of Aran Fawddwy.

6. Continue along the ridge to reach the trig point on Aran Fawddwy (2).

7. Retrace your steps to the last stile that you crossed on the ascent. Do not cross, but turn left and descend, with the fence nearby on the right, to a ladder stile. Now follow a fence on the left to the memorial cairn on Drws-bach (3).

8. Continue along Drws-bach, keeping close to the left fence. At a peaty dip, the path leaves the fence to give fine views over Hengwm.

9. Reach a ladder stile in the fence ahead. Descend with the fence nearby on your left. In about 600 metres, the path leaves the fence and crosses a damp area. Just before the ground rises again, bear right at a post to follow a clear path descending above the valley, Hengwm.

10. Cross a number of streams and stiles. In 2.5km the path becomes fenced. Where there is a gate ahead, bear right on a steep descending path with a fence nearby on your right.

11. Continue along the enclosed path. It bends to the right and passes sheepfolds on your left. Join a broader track, and cross a footbridge.

12. Turn left on the lane, and retrace your steps to the parking area in Cwm Cywarch.

Facilities:

Portaloo at the car park. Pub and camp site in Dinas Mawddwy. Meirion Woollen Mill.

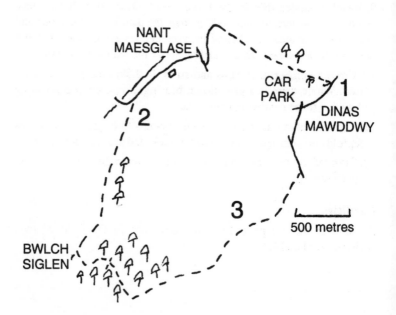

NANT
MAESGLASE

CAR
PARK

1

DINAS
MAWDDWY

2

3

500 metres

BWLCH
SIGLEN

114

Dinas Mawddwy – Red Dragon Mine – Bwlch Siglen – Dyfi Forest – Dinas Mawddwy

OS Maps:	1:50 000 Landranger Sheet 124; 1:25 000 Outdoor Leisure Sheet 23.
Start:	Road junction at the Red Lion in Dinas Mawddwy, G.R. 858148.
Access:	Dinas Mawddwy is just off the A470, 16km east of Dolgellau. Infrequent buses from Dolgellau.
Parking:	Y Plas – about 100 metres from the Red Lion.
Grade:	Moderate – tracks, forest and hill paths.
Time:	3½-4 hours.

Points of Interest:

1. Dinas Mawddwy was the territory of Gwylliaid Cochion Mawddwy ('the Red Bandits of Mawddwy'). On his tour in the 18th century, Thomas Pennant was told that travellers preferred to cross mountain summits on their way to England, rather than take the road. Scythes were placed in chimneys to prevent the bandits entering houses by the rooftops. In 1554, eighty bandits were executed, but the surviving outlaws killed the sheriff responsible for the deaths. They too were caught and executed. When Pennant visited Dinas Mawddwy he saw the stocks and whipping post, but was told that nobody had been whipped for several years. George Borrow, seventy years later, heard sounds of drunken revelry from the huts, and saw fierce looking red haired men staggering about. Lead and slate mining used to be the main industries in the area.

2. The memorial is to Hugh Jones (1749-1825), a Calvinist Methodist hymn writer who lived in the lovely valley of the Nant Maesglase. Higher up the valley, the stream tumbles down Craig Maesglase as a spectacular waterfall. Lead and copper were worked in the Red

Dragon mine, before attempts were made in 1854 to extract gold. Mining was unsuccessful and it closed in 1856.

3. Minllyn quarry employed over 100 men in its extensive open and underground workings. However, it did not have a high output and closed around 1916. Remains include a chimney, a ruined mill and other buildings, and a tramway tunnel leading into a pit. The incline brought material from Cae Abaty quarry, located near the forest. Half a mile east of Minllyn lies a hill slope known as Maes Camlan. It is said to be the site of King Arthur's last battle, when he fought Mordred.

Walk Directions: (-) denotes Point of Interest

1. From the Red Lion *(Y Llew Coch)* in Dinas Mawddwy (1), take the road in the direction of Llanymawddwy. In 400 metres, cross a bridge and turn left on a track which leads into a caravan site.

2. Almost immediately take a track on the right. Go through a field above the site, and follow a fence. Pass through some trees and rhododendrons. Emerge from the trees and bear right on a path, uphill, towards conifers. Cross a broken gate, and turn left on a grassy track.

3. Keep ahead along the track, pass a house and continue on a lane. Bear left at a fork, and cross a bridge. Reach a lane junction and turn left to the main road.

4. Turn right, and in 80 metres, turn left on a lane and follow it for 800 metres. As the lane descends to cross Nant Maesglase, and just before the land bends right, take a level track on the left at a footpath signpost.

5. Pass a monument (2) and go through a gate. Follow the green track along the hillside. Pass a plantation on the left, and cross a stile.

6. The path becomes rougher and crosses a stream. Pass the mine ruins, and continue on a path that slants uphill to the coniferous trees on the skyline.

7. The path becomes fainter just before it reaches the ridge. At Bwlch Siglen it meets another path in front of the forest. Turn left, and in a few paces, cross a stile into the forest.

8. Descend the path through the forest, and in about 120 metres reach a post with yellow arrows. Go left, following a broken wall at first.

9. Emerge on a forest track, and turn left. In a few paces, turn right on a track which narrows to a path. Pass a ruin on the right and look for yellow arrows. About 100 metres beyond the ruin, bear left at a fork in the path.

10. Stay on this path, and bear right with it to cross a stream and stile. Go sharp left, following the forest on your left. Reach some fencing and a stile, cross a stream and bear right, uphill, following the path parallel to the stream.

11. Towards the head of the valley, the path veers left (north), and reaches a plateau. Keep ahead, descending towards the tips of the disused Minllyn slate quarry. Before reaching the quarry, go down into a gully, keep to the right, and follow the incline towards the remains of buildings (3).

12. At the ruins, you will reach a corner fence with arrows. Follow the fence on the right, cross and bear left on a slaty path.

13. Descend with tips on your right, and emerge on another path. Bear right downhill, cross directly over a broad track to a path, and follow it to the A470.

14. Turn left, and shortly go right on a road leading to the Llew Coch in Dinas Mawddwy.

Facilities:

Public toilets near the start. Pub and camp site in Dinas Mawddwy. Meirion Woollen Mill.

Walks with History

If you want to experience the very best of Wales, then these are the books for you. The walks are graded and there is something for everybody – short walks for families and more demanding routes to satisfy even the most experienced hillwalker.

Whether you choose to walk the high grounds, explore the beautiful valleys, study the varied wildlife or visit the remains of ancient castles and forts, the points of interest will explain what makes each area unique and help you choose the right walk for you.

Walks on the Llŷn Peninsula
PART 1 - SOUTH & WEST – N. Burras & J. Stiff.
ISBN 0-86381-343-7; **£4.50**
This series combines walks with history, stories and legends. Pastoral walks as well as coastal & mountain panoramas.

Walks on the Llŷn Peninsula
PART 2 - NORTH & EAST – N. Burras & J. Stiff.
ISBN 0-86381-365-8: **£4.50**

Walks in the Snowdonia Mountains
– Don Hinson. 45 walks, mostly circular, 96 pages, inc. accurate maps and drawings. 96pp ISBN 0-86381-385-2; New Edition: **£3.75**

Walks in North Snowdonia
– Don Hinson. 100km of paths to help those wishing to explore the area further. 96pp ISBN 0-86381-386-0; New Edition; **£3.75**

New Walks in Snowdonia
– Don Hinson. 43 circular walks together with many variations. This book introduces you to lesser known paths and places which guide book writers seem to have neglected. Maps with every walk. Pen & ink drawings.
96pp ISBN 0-86381-390-9; New Edition; **£3.75**

Circular Walks in North Pembrokeshire
– Paul Williams, 14 walks, 112 pages. ISBN 0-86381-420-4; **£4.50**

Circular Walks in South Pembrokeshire
– Paul Williams, 14 walks, 120 pages. ISBN 0-86381-421-2; **£4.50**

From Mountain Tops to Valley Floors
Salter & Worral. ISBN 0-86381-430-1; **£4.50**
Detailed information for casual/family walks and for the more adventurous walker.

WALKS IN WALES - latest titles

Walks from Llandudno
CHRISTOPHER DRAPER
ISBN: 0-86381-559-6; £4.95

Circular Walks in Meirionnydd
DOROTHY HAMILTON
ISBN: 0-86381-545-6; £4.50

Walks in and around the Berwyn Mountains
JOHN TRANTER
ISBN: 0-86381-547-2; £4.50

Circular Walks in North Eastern Wales
JIM GRINDLE
ISBN: 0-86381-550-2; £4.50

The North Wales Path and 10 selected walks
DAVE SALTER & DAVE WORRALL
ISBN: 0-86381-546-4; £4.50

Llŷn Peninsula Coastal Walks
RICHARD QUINN
ISBN: 0-86381-574-X; £4.50

Circular Walks in the Black Mountains
NICK JENKINS
ISBN: 0-86381-558-8; £4.50

Walks in the Wye Valley
RICHARD SALE
ISBN: 0-86381-555-3; £4.50

Circular Walks in the Brecon Beacons National Park;
ISBN 0-86381-476-X; **£4.50**
Circular Walks on Anglesey; ISBN 0-86381-478-6; **£4.50**
Circular Walks in Gower; ISBN 0-86381-479-4; **£4.50**
Circular Walks in Central Wales; ISBN 0-86381-480-8; **£4.50**
Circular Walks in Gwent; ISBN 0-86381-477-8; **£4.50**